BEEN THERE,
GOT THE T-SHIRT

William Webb

Published by
Webb, 2 Wyndthorpe Gardens, Castle Hill, Ilfracombe,
Devon, EX34 9HZ

British Library Cataloguing-in-Publication Data.
A catalogue record for this book is available
from the British Library.

Arthur H. Stockwell Ltd. bears no responsibility
for the accuracy of events recorded in this book.

ISBN 0 9548761 0 5

Printed in Great Britain by
Arthur H. Stockwell Ltd.
Torrs Park   Ilfracombe
Devon

Preface

With aircraft getting bigger and the world seemingly getting smaller, more and more people are travelling overseas for the first time. This modest publication is primarily for their benefit. For forty years I have travelled the globe, mainly in order to earn a crust, but occasionally in pursuit of pleasure, and in that time I have learned a thing or two that have saved me time, money and I suspect even my life on occasions.

For easy reference the book is subdivided into sections entitled; Travelling, Arriving, Accommodation, Health, Culture, Recreation, and Shopping. However, life being what it is, these topics will overlap on occasions so I hope the reader will bear with me if I sometimes meander. This publication is in no way intended to be a reference book, but I hope it will prove useful to both new and seasoned travellers.

William Webb, Devon, 2004

CONTENTS LIST

Chapter one – Travelling
Preparing for the journey   7
The journey   13

Chapter two – Health Care
Medical insurance   27
Precautions   29
Diseases   41
Cholera   41
Hepatitis A & B; Typhoid; Malaria   42
Japanese Encephalitis; Yellow Fever; Rabies   43
Polio; Diphtheria; Meningitis   44
Tetanus; TB; Anthrax; Ebola; Lassa Fever   45
Necrotising Fascitis; Smallpox; Economy Class Syndrome   46
Blood Flow & Constituents; Vein Walls   47
Crime overseas   49
Breaking the law abroad   51

Chapter three – Arriving
The arrival   56
Transportation   58
Car hire   64
Trains   67

Chapter four – Accommodation
Hotels   70
Hotel staff   78
Paying the bill   83
Your holiday rights   85
Airport delays; Missing luggage; Surcharges   85
Overbooking; Tour operator goes bust; Hotel complaints   86

Chapter five – Local Customs and Culture
Offensive words   88
Offensive actions   91
Acceptable dress   96
Humour   98
Treatment of animals   99
Local customs   100
Thumbnail sketches of other travellers   102

Americans   102
Japanese; French   103
Germans   104
Italians   105
Arabs; The Brit abroad   106

Chapter six – Recreation
Drinking abroad   108
Paying for drinks   110
Where to drink   111
Dining out   115
Other pastimes   116

Chapter seven – Shopping
Bartering   122
Places to shop   125
Shopping in the USA   130
Money changing   132
Saving on shopping   134
What, and what not, to buy   135

Appendix
Useful telephone numbers   138
Major airports   138
Car ferry services; Major airlines   139
Useful websites   141

CHAPTER ONE

Travelling

As I climbed into an aircraft for the very first time I was immediately struck by the overpowering stench of vomit. I stood in the aisle and peered into the gloom searching for somewhere to sit, my efforts assisted in no part by the almost complete absence of windows. Having staggered to a vacant seat I sat down and struggled with the safety harness. I was terrified, and recalling that the only two members of my family ever to fly before me had been killed in air crashes did nothing to allay my fears. Admittedly, they had both been shot down over Germany during World War 2, but the fact did nothing to reassure me.

That was fifty years ago when I was a teenager on a Royal Air Force training flight in a Vickers Varsity. Today passengers get on and off aeroplanes just as readily as buses or trains and everyone can tell you that, statistically, flying is by far the safest means of transport. However, boarding an aircraft is not quite as simple as jumping on a bus at the end of the street.

Preparing for the journey
Before departing on any trip it is advisable to plan ahead. I have always been a believer in the maxim *fail to plan, plan to fail.* For every journey it is necessary to carry out a number of mundane tasks such as checking your passport, enquiring whether or not visas are necessary, having the required vaccinations, purchasing a ticket, and packing your case.

If your passport is out of date, or will expire while you are away, it is possible to renew it through selected post office branches and Worldchoice travel agents. They offer a Check and Send service that will do virtually everything for you, for a small remuneration. The Passport Adviceline is 0870 521 0410, or visit *www.passport.gov.uk.*

What goes in the case obviously depends on where and why you are travelling. If flying, a quick perusal of the airline ticket will give an indication of exactly what is, and what is not, permitted to be carried in hand baggage. Items such as weapons, lighter fuel, matches, acid, and bleach, are obviously forbidden, but so are thermometers containing mercury. Christmas crackers are also forbidden but Easyjet are the only company I know of who enforce this rule, although there are possibly others. Most of these items may be carried as cargo subject to certain restrictions.

However, with all the problems of terrorists and hijackings that airlines have to contend with, do not be surprised if the chiming clock picked up in the bazaar finds itself relegated to the hold. I once spent thirty minutes in a stifling hot bus at Beirut Airport as a mauve-rinsed American senior citizen insisted that two loudspeakers carried by a fellow traveller were virtually stripped down to the wires.

It is also recommended you put electrical items such as hair driers and shavers in your hand luggage. In the present climate of high alert security personnel will want to inspect any electrical goods. The last thing you want to do at check-in is to have to open your suitcases to have the contents inspected.

At the height of the Foot and Mouth crisis not too many years ago, the chess correspondent of the *Scotsman* newspaper flew into Seattle Airport with a haggis. It was confiscated immediately by Customs Officers who promptly shot it, threw petrol over it, and then set it alight!

It is also advisable to ascertain exactly what baggage allowance you are entitled to. Carrying excess baggage can work out very expensive. Allowances can vary from airline to airline, and certainly from class to class. For most airlines your allowance is 40 kilos First Class, 30 kilos Business Class, and 20 kilos Economy Class, but it is advisable to check beforehand as allowances do vary.

American Airlines allow Economy Class passengers one piece of hand luggage up to 18 kilos plus a personal item such as a briefcase or handbag. British Airways will only allow you one single item of up to 6 kilos. You can get a 7 kilos allowance with Asia Pacific Airlines, 8 kilos with Lufthansa, and a generous 12 kilos with Air France. These allowances can be as much as trebled by travelling First or Upper Class. There are also size restrictions to be considered so do make sure before you arrive at the airport exactly what your particular airline allows.

If intending to take a mobile phone abroad the first thing to ascertain is that it will work at your intended destination. Your server, Orange, Vodaphone, or whoever, will be able to advise you on this point.

Secondly, be aware that you will have to pay for incoming as well as outgoing calls whilst overseas. Long chats from your daughter on the office phone may cost her nothing but will certainly cost you. Text messages can cost you up to 600% more than at home. Get a plug adapter for your charger if going to Europe, or a different charger if you are going somewhere where the local supply is 110 volts. Finally, and most importantly, pack your phone in your hand baggage so that you can ensure it is not switched on in flight. Transmissions from switched-on phones can cause havoc to an aircraft's electronic systems.

Phone theft on the continent is not as rife as in Britain but it is still worthwhile to be cautious when using your mobile. Before you leave on your journey record your phone's IMEI number (key *#06# to find out what it is). This will enable you to prove it is yours or to disable it if stolen. It is also advisable to use the PIN code security lock. Very recently a couple living quite close to me in Devon had their mobile phone stolen while on holiday in Africa. The thief had run up a bill of many hundreds of pounds within a couple of hours before they were able to put a stop on it.

On the subject of luggage, there is no definite way to ensure that it will not go astray. I recently booked in at Heathrow with four pieces of luggage. Three items and myself arrived safely in Dhaka, Bangladesh, the fourth went on to Melbourne, Australia. Fortunately, with the use of a computerised luggage search programme, it was returned to me three weeks later. There are, however, ways of cutting down the odds against losing one's luggage. A mass of hotel labels festooning a bag may seem ostentatious, but it does help ensure that at the end of the journey it will not accidentally be picked up by a fellow passenger. In the present climate of mass produced foreign imports it is not unusual to see half a dozen people leap forward to grab the same piece of Samsonite luggage from the carousel. Just one easily recognised label in a prominent position will facilitate the recognition of one's own property. Another added bonus is that a shabby-looking item of luggage is less likely to appeal to any would-be thieves.

A simple way of reducing the effect of lost luggage is to split the load between two cases. If travelling as a couple, do not pack separate suitcases but put half of your belongings in each case. If travelling alone carry two smaller cases in preference to one large one. Put half the shirts in each case, half the socks, pants, shoes, etc. That way you will at least have a complete set of clothes to wear if a case is lost, and the chance of losing both cases has to be less likely.

Another novel idea if going on holiday is to just pack all your oldest clothes, towels, almost empty perfume and aftershave bottles, etc., and discard everything after use. That way you clear a lot of rubbish from home, probably make a few of the locals happy, and have plenty of room for presents and duty free goods on the way home.

A piece of advice given to me long ago was, when preparing to travel, lay out all your clothes and money beforehand, then half the clothes and double the money. It is always simple to halve the clothes but coming up with twice the money can be tricky.

I have been luckier than most. I travelled for thirty years without any mishap at all regarding luggage then lost it twice in 1991, thankfully, again only temporarily.

The unluckiest man I ever met was Al Waifer, an American ex-Vietnam pilot I had the pleasure of working with in Libya. He had lost his luggage so many times that he was genuinely surprised to find his bag waiting for him when he disembarked.

On one occasion we booked in together at Benghazi Airport, watched our two bags get tagged together, watched them disappear together into the baggage hall, climbed on the aircraft and sat side by side for the thirty minute flight to Tripoli, only to discover on arriving that my bag had made it, Al's had not!

Although sticking labels on one's cases may be a good idea, leaving airline destination tags on them is definitely not. It may help to impress fellow travellers, always assuming they know where HRE, VFA, and GBE are, but it can lead to the luggage making a return trip to exotic places without its owner.

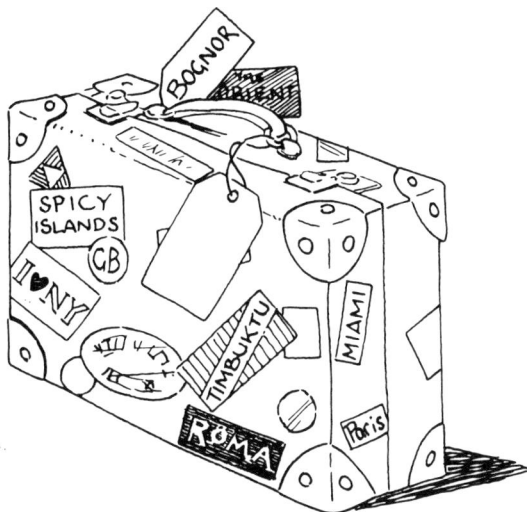

Should your luggage inadvertently go astray it would facilitate its return if your home address is available. It is obviously a good idea to have a label with this information on it either inside the case, or on a luggage tag outside the case. The problem with having the information inside the luggage is that it will probably be necessary to damage the locks in order to obtain it. It is, therefore, advisable to have your address readily available outside the case. If outside this should not be on view to all and sundry. The last thing you want to do is to advise any would-be burglar of your home address and the fact that you are going to be away for a week or two.

Keep your address hidden inside a luggage tag otherwise you could return to find your home stripped bare. I recall a case at a certain UK airport where the young woman on the check-in counter was convicted of passing on information to her brother who, with an accomplice, would then ransack the empty houses. It was quite simple for her, in the guise of being friendly, to ask passengers how long they were going to be away, while at the same time memorising the address on their cases as she fitted the baggage tags.

I use a Barclaycard security tag on my baggage which means my personal details are not evident to anyone and yet allows lost luggage to be traced, as was proven when my case made its way back from Australia.

If you are unlucky enough to lose your luggage remember, besides claiming from your insurance, you may also be able to claim an immediate payment from the airline for emergency purchases. Some credit card companies will also pay you for lost luggage. With an American Express Gold Card you may claim up to £750 if your baggage is six hours late, and up to £1,000 after a further forty-eight hours, as long as you have used the card to purchase your ticket.

The procedure to follow if you are unfortunate enough to lose your luggage is to report it immediately to the airline staff or the Customer Services desk before leaving the baggage reclaim area. You will then be requested to complete a Property Irregularity Report (PIR). You will need a copy of this and your baggage tags to claim against the airline or your insurance. You must then claim in writing from the airline concerned.

Damaged luggage must be reported within seven days and missing luggage within twenty-one days otherwise your claim will be considered null and void. Until July 2004, airlines had only to pay £14 per kilo for lost luggage under the Warsaw Convention of 1929, unless, of course, you were a well-known pop star married to an equally well-known footballer. However, under the new Montreal Convention, travellers may now claim up to £850 compensation. A total of fifty-four countries signed up to the new agreement including the USA and all EU member states, but beware if travelling on certain African airlines as the new rules do not apply to them. Your flight ticket will tell you whether or not your carrier has signed up to the Montreal Convention.

There is, however, a drawback to the new regulations. In the past, because compensation payments were so low, airlines invariably paid up on demand. In the future they are not going to be so quick to pay out. The onus will be upon the passenger to prove what they claim was in the lost suitcase really was there. You may be required to provide receipts of everything that was lost. British Airways says that it carries around 50 million items of luggage a year of which about 5,000 are permanently lost. You could find yourself in a long queue for compensation. Your best bet it still to buy travel insurance that covers you and your baggage.

Make sure that your luggage is securely fastened. A lock on the zip of a holdall is no deterrent to a determined thief, as I found out at

Lagos Airport when an expensive frequency counter was removed without any damage to the bag. Arriving at Dhaka recently I was amazed at the ropes and straps securing the baggage of the local population. I soon realised why when my travelling companion pointed out his bag had been rifled on its way from the aircraft to the terminal building.

If travelling off to lesser-known destinations, i.e. anywhere outside Europe, the USA, and the Antipodes, it is always worth making a call to the Foreign Office to check whether or not anything untoward has happened or is expected to happen. Civil unrest can erupt with amazing speed in Africa, South America, and Asia. I have personally been involved in riotous actions in Nigeria, Zimbabwe, and Bangladesh. Fortunately, only my vehicle was damaged but it is not unknown for innocent bystanders to suffer serious injury, or worse.

Finally, and this applies equally when returning to the UK, never carry anything for anyone else unless you can trust them explicitly, and even then think carefully. I have been approached at many airports by respectable looking people and asked to post packages back in the UK "for my mother's birthday", "my son's Christmas present", etc., and have always refused. If the person asking is a genuine expatriate then they will fully understand your reluctance to carry the goods.

When first working in Riyadh and there were only a dozen or so of us, it was quite normal to carry home a pile of mail to post at Heathrow, especially at Christmas time. The mail would also include cassettes as some of the technicians preferred to send audio rather than written messages. This practice came to an abrupt halt after a Customs Officer opened a package and discovered one of the cassettes actually contained gold jewellery. The unfortunate, innocent carrier spent three hours at Heathrow being questioned and waiting whilst every packet was opened and checked. Fortunately, the would-be smuggler was not too bright and had addressed the package to himself at his home address so was easily traced, and charged.

The journey
Wear layers of light clothing when flying, they are easier to discard should the temperature get a bit warm inside the aircraft. Bulky items are awkward to shed and even more awkward to stow away in flight. Loose shoes are also a good idea as most passengers' feet swell from the effects of low air pressure.

So, having safely packed the bags, dressed sensibly, and arrived at the check-in desk at least one hour before take-off (two hours before if flying El Al), it is advisable to know in advance where you wish to be seated. Most airlines have a seating plan available at the check-in desk so it is a simple matter to determine what seats are smoking or non-smoking, on the aisle, near a window, or near an emergency exit if you are a nervous flier. It is a little more difficult to discover which seats have the extra legroom or whether or not you will have a good view of the screen should an in-flight movie be shown. My own priorities are simple; easy access to the drinks trolley and the toilet.

Above your seat will be a control unit with a reading light switch, a call button, and a fresh air control. A little common sense should tell you not to have the reading light on if the rest of the aircraft are watching an in-flight movie, and not to attempt to call the cabin staff during take-off and landing, or when meals are being served.

Also above your seat will be an overhead locker for storing your hand luggage, coat, duty free goods, etc. Be very careful how you stow items in the locker because they will get thrown about when in flight. Be even more careful when you come to open up again. I have lost count of the number of times I have seen objects tumble out as soon as the locker catch is pressed. Your fellow passengers will not appreciate being struck by a bottle of wine whatever vintage it may be.

Flying definitely has a dehydrating effect so it is advisable to drink reasonable amounts of non-alcoholic liquids. Drinking water can be obtained from dispensers on Boeing 747s, DC 10s, and TriStars. Cabin staff will also provide free soft drinks on most flights.

Many airlines use similar aircraft such as the Boeing 747, Boeing 737, and the Airbus A-300, but not all interiors are the same. Charter aircraft will usually be less generous than the major airlines when it comes to allocating space. In almost every aeroplane there have to be some seats that do not recline making long journeys most uncomfortable for the unlucky passenger in such a seat. On charter flights you are more likely to come across non-reclining seats. The airlines are not obliged to inform passengers on checking in that the seat they have been allocated is non-reclining, but will admit it if they are asked.

If you stipulate a reclining seat or one with extra legroom at time of booking do not be surprised if you are asked to pay extra to ensure your request is granted.

I was fortunate enough to have done the bulk of my travelling before terrorism became the issue that it is today. With the introduction of Air Marshals I suppose there are going to be certain seats that are no longer available to the travelling public, probably at the rear of Economy Class. There would not be much point in having them sat in the front row of First Class where they would not be able to see any action going on behind them.

I must confess I am not happy with the idea of having some gung ho Yank, armed to the teeth, sitting behind me. As far as I am concerned he is there for one reason only; to ensure that no hijacked aircraft ever again arrives over US territory. How he ensures this I leave to your imagination.

However, I digress, to return to the matter in hand, it also pays to be polite at the check-in desk. Remember, the person checking you in can determine whether or not you pass the journey sat next to an attractive member of the opposite sex, or a nursing mother with a bad-tempered infant.

Generally, I have found check-in staff the world over to be extremely courteous, patient, and willing to help with information as to what seats are most suitable for one's requirements.

Mostly your choice of airline is determined by your destination. For example, there are not too many choices if you wish to fly to Moshoeshoe in Lesotho, Entebbe in Uganda, or Khamis Mushait in Saudi Arabia. When a choice is available it pays to shop about. Fares can differ enormously from one airline to another. Fares for the same flight can also vary quite dramatically depending on where and when the ticket is acquired. Fares for the same journey can also vary dramatically according to how you are travelling.

British Airways have a wide variety of different tariffs; First Class, Club World, World Traveller, etc., but if only going on holiday once a year you are better sticking to good old Economy Class. This still gives you an opportunity to shop about. So called "bucket shops" can save you pounds especially if your itinerary is flexible. The *"Exchange and Mart"* is an ideal place to look for bargain flights, as is the Internet at such sites as *deckchair.com* and *lastminute.com.* Travel agents also have "last minute offers" if you are prepared to fly off at short notice.

If booking over the telephone make sure you write down all the details and then check them again when the confirmation/tickets arrive. We have all heard the old chestnut of how a message sent as "send reinforcements, going to advance", was received as "send three and fourpence, going to a dance", but getting tickets to Dakar, Senegal when you wished to go to Dhaka, Bangladesh is not as amusing.

Wherever you book your flight or holiday make sure the company selling you the ticket is a member of one of the established bonding schemes; ABTA (Association of British Travel Agents), AITO (Association of Independent Tour Operators), or ATOL (Air Travel Organiser's Licence). Not only is your flight/holiday guaranteed should the company go bankrupt, but there are also arbitration schemes should you have any complaints about the treatment received.

The "no frills" airlines such as Ryanair, Easyjet, Debonair, Virgin

Express, and BA's Go can offer vastly reduced prices on some of the popular routes. For example, at time of going to press, a return ticket London — Nice will cost £198 on a British Midland flight but only £80 on Easyjet. As with everything else in life, on a "no frills" flight you get what you pay for, and some of the things you have not paid for are a meal during the flight, an assigned seat, and free drinks.

You are also not issued with a ticket at time of purchase, you pick up a boarding pass on checking in at the time of the flight. Furthermore, you do not have the right to change or cancel the flight, and there are no refunds. Another problem is that the "no frills" airlines tend to use the less expensive airfields such as Luton and Stansted near London, and Beauvais near Paris which are at a far greater distance from town than Heathrow, Orly, or Charles De Gaulle.

Business passengers may find the money saved on the flight is gobbled up by the taxi fare to get them to their meetings in time. There is, of course, no connection to international flights at most of the cheaper airfields and the punctuality of a lot of "no frills" airlines leaves a lot to be desired.

Ryanair recently announced that their next generation of aircraft will have even less "frills". There will be no reclining seats, no headrests, no window blinds, and possible restriction of baggage size. They are even contemplating doing away with unaccompanied luggage altogether. Only hand luggage will be allowed, which enables the airline to do away with all baggage-handling facilities. How a family with three children will be expected to go on a fortnight's holiday with just carrier bags as luggage defeats me. What about babies' buggies and carrycots? Are they expected to go on board with the passengers? Has the question of wheelchairs been considered?

The "no frills" airlines may be cheap but to me they are anything but cheerful.

If a scheduled flight is overbooked and you find yourself bumped off, remember you can claim compensation under EEC law. The amount of compensation depends on the length of the flight. I seem to recall about £250 for a long-haul journey.

No matter how you fly, scheduled airlines or "no frills", to get the best bargains it is advisable, if possible, to travel midday, midweek, and midwinter!

Having spent many years flying to different parts of the globe I have compiled my own private league of airlines. My all-time favourite is KLM, the Dutch airline. They cover most of the world but keep up their very high standard no matter where they operate. Some airlines' standards appear to be inversely proportional to the distance from home base; i.e. the greater the distance, the lower the standard.

Second in my league is Swissair, but I must admit that British Airways, at present lying third, are improving all the time. Some years ago I would even suffer the trauma of going the extra miles to Gatwick to catch a British Caledonian flight rather than use BA to Nigeria, but now use them regularly. Air Maroc are my favourite African airline, although I have no complaints with South African Airways.

Libyan Airlines are the only airline I know of that still offer boiled sweets to passengers on take-off and landing. This, however, is small recompense for the fact that no alcohol is served throughout the flight. As the aircraft climbs out from Tripoli Airport with the American Sixth Fleet patrolling menacingly below, there are times when a stiff drink would not go amiss. However, as I believe sanctions are no longer in force against the Socialist Peoples' Libyan Arab Jahamariyah, maybe I will soon once again be able to enjoy a boiled sweet on Libyan Airlines.

Nigeria Airways are indisputably bottom of my private league. The area around the check-in desk at Lagos Mutallah Muhammed Airport can sometimes resemble a battlefield. I have seen soldiers using rifle butts in an attempt to restore order. The problem is the age-old one of "dash" (see chapter 5). An OK ticket is not worth a light if there is someone prepared to pay to board the aircraft, and there always is.

Having succeeded in boarding a Nigerian Airways aircraft one's problems are not over, quite the contrary. One afternoon I was strapped in my seat on a Fokker Friendship F27 at Ibadan Airport waiting for the engines to start up when there was a violent banging on the side of the aircraft. Oh God! I thought, not another political coup. I had just experienced my third in as many years. After a few moments of frantic pounding a steward got out of his seat and opened the main door. I was very relieved not to find myself looking down the barrel of an automatic rifle, but rather alarmed to see I was looking into the face of the pilot. What he said on boarding is unrepeatable, but to say he was not amused at being locked out of his own aircraft is an understatement.

Flying is undoubtedly the safest means of transport but this does not prevent some people from being nervous whenever they take to the air. If flying British Airways you can be assured that the pilots are top rate. Twice a year every BA pilot has to attend a Flight Training centre for a two-day flight simulator session where for four hours each day his flying skills are tested to the limit. He is also subjected, once a year, to an unannounced in-flight route check where once again his every action is scrutinised. Furthermore, he has to pass two strict medicals every year. What a pity car drivers are not treated similarly; there would be a lot more room on the roads!

For would-be travellers with a distinct phobia of flying there are several courses run around the country to help you overcome your fear. Virgin Atlantic run a one-day Flying Without Fear course (01423 71490) where Virgin pilots explain everything to do with the flight. This includes a quick course on aerodynamics, navigation, and engines, and a question and answer session. This is followed by lunch and a flight. These are held at Gatwick or Manchester and cost around £200.

Aviators Fly Without Fear (01252 793250) is a BA run course at Heathrow with British Airways pilots, costing slightly less than Virgin.

Flying Fear is run at Exeter and Birmingham and is a one-day course that includes a thirty-minute flight, always assuming you pass the course! At a total cost of £165 this seems a bargain to me.

Britannia Airways run Flying With Confidence at East Midlands Airport for around £175.

All of the above courses can be found on the web and are listed in the appendix to this book.

Even the best of aircrews are not above the odd practical joke. I have heard of cases where, on having a newly qualified flight attendant on board, the crew of the flight deck have feigned airsickness and asked the young lady for sick bags. When she has left the flight deck they have emptied a tin of warm vegetable soup into the bags then recalled her to collect them. What the poor girl thought of it all I dread to think.

Even more vindictive crews have been known to smear melted chocolate around the toilet pan and walls of the first class toilet then complained bitterly to the new girl about the state of the place! And I thought air force initiation ceremonies were vicious.

One commercial pilot I met who had, incidentally, failed in his attempt to join BA, told me of a training flight where the captain had backed out of the cockpit trailing two pieces of string. These he had handed to an old lady sitting in the first row of the passenger seats, placing one piece in each hand. He convinced the poor old soul she was guiding the aircraft and told her that she had to hold it steady as he was desperate to use the toilet. He then disappeared for almost ten minutes in which time she must have aged ten years.

If you are the nervous type you may like to know that in 1998 aircraft from Gambia, Haiti, Honduras, Malta, Paraguay, Swaziland, Uruguay, and Zimbabwe were banned from flying into the USA. I have personally flown on three of the aforementioned airlines and lived to tell the tale. If you are concerned you can always visit the *www.airsafe.com* website and review the latest situation. At time of going to press Australasian airlines averaged 3 million flight hours between major accidents, US airlines 2 million hours, but South America, Central Africa, and Asia only 350,000 hours.

Before take-off you will be given instructions on what to do in an emergency. This is either given over the intercom with a practical demonstration by one of the cabin staff, or more likely on a modern aircraft, by means of a videotape. Various things are explained such as the use of the emergency exits and the oxygen masks. I have been flying for fifty years and, fortunately, have never had to use either.

I never cease to be amazed at the number of passengers who immediately reach for a newspaper or magazine as soon as one of the cabin crew commences a safety talk. This "I don't need to listen, I've flown before" attitude does not impress any more as the whole world and his brother have flown before. And I am willing to bet that in more cases than not the person concerned has not flown on that particular model of aircraft before. The Boeing 747 has at least fifteen models that I know of, and that does not include specials such as the ones that ferry space shuttles between Florida and California. I always listen otherwise you could miss gems like, "We are now going to show you a safety video. There may be fifty ways to leave your lover but only six ways to leave this aircraft."

I must admit there are times when I wish I had not read somewhere that a modern aircraft contains more than 6 million separate parts and that it takes 75,000 engineering drawings to put them all together. I am also nervous of the fact that modern aircraft are completely designed on computers, especially knowing the fact that if one feeds in the dimensions of a bumble bee to a computer, it will tell you that it will never fly!

During the safety talk the adoption of the "crash position" is also explained. This entails bending forward and curling yourself into a tight ball with the hands tucked under the legs. I have heard of three different explanations for this particular position. One, in the event of a crash the spine is forced up through the brain thereby ensuring a swift departure from this mortal coil. Two, it helps preserve passengers' teeth to help identification later. Three, it is the ideal position in which to kiss one's arse goodbye (courtesy of the RAF). The truth is, that it is the safest position to adopt as it prevents one's limbs being flung about haphazardly on impact.

Airlines, in an effort to expand their part of the market are constantly coming up with innovations and free offers, such as a hire car for twenty-four hours by Gulf Air. Some offers available are welcome and some are quite frankly, ridiculous. For example, Qantas, the

Australian airline, now have windows in their first class toilets. I expect there to be a complaint from the Women's Lib lobby at any time as it is blatantly obvious that only the male passengers are in a position to enjoy the view while partaking of this particular amenity. Quite frankly I have always been too busy concentrating on maintaining my balance to worry about what particular cloud is now passing the aircraft. And for the life of me I cannot fathom why the window is fitted with a pull down shade. Even on the ground a man would have to be thirty feet tall to look in the window and who the heck is hanging about at thirty thousand feet waiting to take a peek?

While on the subject, beware when flushing the pan after use. In 2002, an American female passenger on an SAS (Scandinavian Airlines) Boeing 747 bound for New York decided to flush before standing up. The resulting powerful vacuum action then held her fast. The cabin crew were unable to free her so the unfortunate woman spent the rest of the journey stuck firmly to the toilet. It took the combined efforts of cabin crew and New York ground staff to eventually free her.

Virgin Atlantic, undisputed leader in the gimmick stakes with free transport to and from the airport, on board pub, Shiatsu massage, etc., is now considering the availability of double beds in private mini cabins. The Mile High Club will soon have more members than the Manchester United Supporters' Club.

British Airways have a Tuck Shop facility for Business Class passengers. Having stuffed themselves on company expenses while abroad, the would-be fatties can now enjoy the return home, and a return to childhood, stuffing themselves with chocolate bars and jelly babies. While on the subject of childhood, in Economy Class on BA children are fed first and given a bag of toys.

Singapore Airlines have a free phone facility between seats. I have still to fathom out what possible benefit this can be to the normal passenger. I think any attractive female will be put off travelling Singapore Airlines knowing that on an eight hour flight across the world she is likely to be subjected to a constant barrage of calls from increasingly drunken, lecherous men. This is definitely not one of the better gimmicks.

Air Jamaica has on-board aerobics and in-flight fashion shows. Not my cup of tea but to each his own.

Airport Tax is something to be wary of. There seems no rhyme or reason for it other than to fill governments' coffers. Even the UK has finally sunk to this desperate measure to grab money from the weary traveller. The most efficient airport on earth, Schipol in Amsterdam, does not fleece its customers this way. Be aware when arriving at foreign airports that some, such as Entebbe and Nairobi, insist on being paid in US dollars or sterling and will only accept cash, not travellers' cheques.

It was at Lagos Airport catching a London bound flight, that I came to the rescue of a member of the Cherubims and Seraphims religious order. She was a very large lady dressed completely in white from her hat to her shoes, and I came across her in an extremely distressed state pleading with an immigration official to allow her onto the aircraft for which she had the appropriate boarding card. Unfortunately she did not have any money with which to pay the Airport Tax.

She had been seen off by her relatives, to whom she had given the last of her Nigerian currency, before returning to London where she had lived for a number of years. Unfortunately, no one had reminded her that she would need niara to pay the Airport Tax before she was allowed to leave the country.

She faced a long journey back into Lagos to get money from a relative plus the hassle and expense of rebooking a flight. As only a few niara were involved I stepped in and paid her tax, much to the disgust of the immigration official who would have probably ended up with the woman's rings and watch as payment.

I was rather embarrassed by her profuse thanks and her exclamations that I would get my reward in Heaven. When flying with Nigerian Airways the last thing I wanted to be reminded of was the hereafter.

It is a good idea to obtain a little of the currency of whatever country you are visiting before departure. On arrival you may need a little cash to pay the porter or for a taxi if not being met at the airport. Do not carry too much as it is invariably cheaper to buy the currency once you arrive in the country.

One final thing, before setting off to catch your aircraft make sure you have all the necessary documents, i.e. current passport, a visa if necessary, and inoculations for the country or countries that you are visiting. Your local health centre or GP will be able to advise you on what is required. Having once travelled without the necessary documentation and subsequently found myself being inoculated in an African clinic, I can assure you that it is a lot less traumatic being given your jabs in the UK. Also make certain that you have a holiday insurance to cover you in case of illness or loss of personal effects. It could be the best investment you ever make.

It pays to read the small print on travel insurance policies as some companies are loathe to pay out when one does have cause to claim.

In 1994, after having to fly back to the UK from Botswana to attend the funeral of my mother I was informed by the insurance company that my mother did not qualify as a "close relative". This term only applied to my wife and children. After weeks of wrangling the company reluctantly agreed to reimburse me for half the cost of the ticket. I received nothing for hotel bills, hire cars, etc. And this was a company I had dealt with for a considerable time on a regular basis.

Another thing worth remembering is, if, for no fault of your own, you arrive late at the airport and miss your flight you may find the insurance company will not pay up if you arrived at the airport by taxi or private car. Many policies state they are only liable if *public transport* lets you down.

Although it is possible to select what airline to fly with, and even to a certain extent what kind of aircraft to fly on, the thing over which you have no control are the other passengers. Flying First Class across the Atlantic is certainly no guarantee of genial company. I was fortunate enough to have had the company of Mr Danny La Rue on my last Upper Class Virgin flight from Miami, but it is possible to find a drunken rock band hurling beer cans around the First Class cabin. On flights to other locations you are likely to come across high-spirited football, rugby, or cricket teams, every one of which has a member who thinks he is irresistible to the stewardesses on board.

By far and away the nicest passengers are usually found in Economy, but if you are not overfond of other peoples' children keep clear of "lollipop specials". These are flights at the beginning and end of school holidays that transport expatriates' children to and from wherever their parents happen to be.

The kids are usually in a high state of excitement and not prone to sitting still for hours on end. However, I recollect on one occasion flying back from Kuwait on a Gulf Air flight with three delightful children who kept me constantly amused with riddles, jokes, noughts and crosses, and card games while their mother slept exhausted in a seat across the aisle. I was amazed how quickly the six hours passed before we were preparing to descend into Heathrow.

If travelling with young children, remember even a two-hour flight is a long time for a normal child to sit still and most airlines take a dim view of young children dashing up and down the aisles. Make sure you take something to keep them amused. Board games, unless of a magnetic variety, are a non starter but almost any card game is quite practical and takes up no more space than a packet of cigarettes.

Club, or Business Class passengers are usually too preoccupied with forthcoming, or just completed meetings to indulge in niceties so this is the ideal way to travel if you wish not to be disturbed. Even the cabin staff will ignore you, unlike in First Class/Upper Class where they are constantly pestering you to partake of refreshments.

Be considerate to the wishes and comfort of other passengers. Do not switch the overhead air conditioning control to maximum then direct the jet in someone else's direction, unless he/she is one of those confounded pests, usually foreign, who insist on smoking in a non-smoking area.

I was extremely fortunate in that I did the bulk of my travelling before "air rage" became fashionable. I was absolutely amazed to read that in the first three months of the year 2003 there were 648 incidents of so called air rage reported worldwide. These were termed "significant" incidents that were duly reported. The number of unreported incidents is anybody's guess.

Fortunately, the authorities have acted very quickly to stamp out this kind of behaviour and under the new Aviation Offences Act the maximum sentence for endangering the safety of an aircraft has been raised from two to five years.

Strangely enough, although it is alcohol that is the biggest problem, 42% of incidents, it is smoking that accounts for most disturbances, albeit, only 40% serious. The typical enraged passenger has been described as a man thirty-five to forty-five, travelling alone, in Economy Class. As a contractor, this description fitted me perfectly for ten years of my life during which I was an ideal passenger. And I've never smoked a cigarette in my life!

Having patience is definitely a virtue when flying, but there are occasions when even the most patient amongst us are put to the test. On a recent trip I was rerouted through Gatwick to Tunisia at the last moment. Now I have nothing against Gatwick, it is a well organised and efficient airport, but, as I live in Devon it riles me somewhat to have to drive past Heathrow to catch an aircraft a further thirty or forty miles down the road.

I had caught the train from Tiverton Parkway at four minutes past midnight and spent an hour freezing at Reading Station, so I was not exactly at my best when I clambered on the aircraft at half past eight in the morning. On finding someone already sat in my seat I politely informed him he was sat in the wrong place.

"Oh no he's not!" emphatically stated a brassy blonde harridan who was sat beside him "we are all together." She obviously included a replica of herself sat in the window seat in this statement. I double-checked my boarding pass.

"In that case, madam," I informed her, "you must all be sat in the wrong seats."

By this time we had attracted the attention of almost everyone in

Business Class and, fortunately, one of the stewardesses. After checking my boarding pass she politely informed the woman that I did indeed hold the ticket for seat 7D. A quick check of their boarding passes revealed all three were supposed to be sat in Economy Class, to where they were swiftly escorted.

I glanced at my watch as I settled wearily into my seat; we were already two minutes late in taking off. A highly flustered, middle-aged couple suddenly appeared in the gangway and made their way into the two spare seats beside me. Once again I sat back in my seat hoping we could soon take off as I had just one hour between landing at Tunis and catching my connecting flight to Djerba.

The familiar "bing bong" on the intercom warned of an impending announcement.

"Good morning. This is your captain speaking. I must apologise for a further delay in our take-off, but the catering department have failed to deliver special diets."

I could tell by the tone of his voice he was as cheesed off as I was.

"Oh Hell!" I exclaimed to the man sat beside me, "because some health freak wants to eat rabbit food I shall miss my connecting flight." I slumped back in my seat and resigned myself to the fact that I would have to fight my way through a horde of tourists to get myself on the standby list at Tunis Airport.

We eventually took off almost fifteen minutes late and half an hour after that the galley carts were wheeled out.

"Two vegetarian meals?" enquired the stewardess handing them to the couple sat next to me. Well, I had been up all night.

Flying has the strangest affect on some people and ethnic background apparently has a lot to do with it. The Jews appear to be very nervous air passengers. Every El Al flight seems to have at least two rabbis on board who stand at the rear of the aircraft and proceed to conduct a service throughout the flight, making a trip to the toilet all the more difficult for non-believers.

The Arabs all become nomadic as soon as the "seat belts on" sign disappears. They rise up en masse and wander around the aircraft greeting friends and acquaintances. They are also notorious for smoking wherever they go, whether or not the airline permits it.

Islamic passengers heading to Mecca on the Haj have to be watched extremely closely. Many of them have spent a lifetime saving for the pilgrimage that is an essential part of the Islamic faith, and are flying for the first time. It is not unheard of for a pilgrim to retrieve a primus stove from his hand luggage and proceed to brew up in the aisle of the aeroplane. It is strongly rumoured in aviation circles that a similar act was responsible for a Saudair jumbo jet bursting into flames at Riyadh

Airport with extensive loss of life. Other Haj flight passengers have been known to attempt to open an emergency door looking for the toilet.

Americans are the ones most likely to applaud the captain and crew. After a particularly bumpy flight and a landing in atrocious weather I have observed almost every passenger on a US internal airline clap and cheer loudly as the wheels have safely touched down. The only time I have witnessed anything similar on a British aircraft was at Harare in 1991. A starboard engine on a British Airways 747 had burst into flames on take-off and we spent the best part of two hours flying around Zimbabwe on three engines dumping tons of fuel while the offending engine glowed ominously in the pitch darkness. On arriving back at the airport and touching down safely there was a huge cheer from the passengers; I may even have cheered myself!

Individuals of any nationality can be guilty of peculiar behaviour when flying. On a South African bound flight in 1984 I was amazed when a fellow passenger emerged from the toilet resplendent in paisley-patterned pyjamas. It transpired he was an Irishman flying to Zimbabwe as part of the ODA Aid Programme so presumably he was quite normal.

My own daughter, when quite young, on a trip to Nigeria, found herself sitting next to a large German frau. The woman wolfed her own in-flight meal then turned her attention to Nicola's.

"You no vant?" she enquired, indicating the dish of salad my daughter had pushed aside. The slightest shake of Nicola's head was enough, the salad was snatched and rapidly disposed of. The same thing occurred with every dish she pushed aside. Before the next meal was served I changed seats with my daughter as I was quite certain she had given half her meal away out of sheer terror.

On an Egypt Air flight from Lagos to Cairo I sat beside an old black woman who stuffed every item of cutlery down the front of her dress and then proceeded to eat the meal of chicken and rice with her fingers. The airlines have no objections to passengers keeping the menu as a souvenir but they do object to people stealing the cutlery.

On another Egypt Air flight from Cairo to London I had the pleasure of sitting next to a very attractive Egyptian lady. As we approached Heathrow Airport she withdrew a pair of stockings from her handbag and proceeded to put them on, thereby exposing a large expanse of shapely thigh as she did so. She informed me that it had been too hot to wear them in Egypt, but that her husband would expect her to be wearing stockings when she arrived in England.

I have to confess that I have myself been guilty of behaviour that could only have been described as peculiar by an observer unaware of the circumstances. In Libya all announcements and notices, including those at airports, are only given in Arabic, no other language is tolerated. On my travels I have picked up a bit of the language, enough to say "good day", "goodbye", "thank you", "how much" and suchlike, but not enough to understand a rapidly given instruction that my flight was now boarding at such and such a gate.

I had, therefore, carefully formulated a plan whereby I would watch an Arab passenger book onto the same flight as myself, then strategically place myself in the departure lounge where I would keep an eye on him. When he stood up to board the aircraft I would follow on with my boarding pass clutched in my hand. This plan worked perfectly until the day I booked in behind an old gent who evidently had trouble with his waterworks. Having followed him to the toilet on three separate occasions, much to his annoyance and my embarrassment, when he arose for the forth time I sat firm, and promptly missed the flight to Benghazi.

Airlines, and not before time in my opinion, have now begun to scrutinise hand luggage more closely. Make sure you do not exceed your permitted limit that differs according to class of ticket and also from airline to airline.

The definition of hand luggage varies from country to country. The Americans often carry aboard bags large enough to hold three dress suits hanging on a rail that they then attempt to stuff into the overhead lockers. Most Africans carry cases the size of coffins that they force under the seats making it virtually impossible for anyone in the same row to get out to go to the toilet.

The Filipinos, however, take the cake. I have sat watching at Dhahran Airport and seen them staggering on board a Philippines Airways jet carrying TVs, video recorders, electric fans, and even refrigerators. I have often wondered where on earth they stow them whilst in flight; the gangways must be impassable.

Well, by now you should know a little more about packing and labelling your luggage and what to expect when you board the aircraft. However, what awaits you at the end of your journey? In a later chapter I will attempt to describe what may await you at your destination, and hopefully give a few tips on how to avoid disaster.

Airsmiles 1

A naïve young woman was due to fly for the first time. She telephoned the travel agent to ask how long would it take to fly from Birmingham to Majorca.

"Just a minute" said the voice on the phone.

"Thank you" replied the woman as she hung up.

CHAPTER TWO

Health Care

Medical insurance

I suppose the best advice one can give about hospitals is stay out of them. This applies equally to the UK as anywhere else.

As mentioned earlier, no one should contemplate travelling abroad without some kind of insurance cover. Now we are committed members of the EEC we are informed that reciprocal medical care is available in some countries on the continent — whatever that may mean. I think, in essence, it says that if you can prove the food poisoning you are suffering from was definitely caused by your visit to a local restaurant you can visit the local hospital and risk adding septicaemia to your problems.

There is a very useful booklet available that is published by the department of Health entitled *Health Advice for Travellers*. This publication also includes a copy of Form E111 that, having been completed and stamped at the post office, will in a lot of cases entitle you to free or reduced-cost emergency treatment. It also contains a lot of useful information regarding what diseases are to be found at various locations, and what precautions are necessary, or recommended. To obtain a free copy first try your local post office, if unsuccessful there telephone 0800 555 777 at any time free of charge. It is a frighteningly efficient service, all that is required is your postcode and house number!

On the subject of numbers, the emergency number for any EEC country and also for Estonia, Iceland, Liechtenstein, Norway, Slovenia, and Turkey is 112. Unfortunately, this number connects to different emergency services in different countries. In Belgium, Corsica, and Germany 112 gets you the fire brigade. In Italy it's the police. In the USA the emergency number is 911.

Medical treatment varies enormously from country to country. I have been inside foreign hospitals that would not meet the requirements set for abattoirs in the UK. Also, costs can vary enormously.

I was unfortunate enough to have contracted food poisoning after eating half-cooked scampi in a restaurant in Rochester, New York some years ago. A fellow Brit, staying in the next cabin at the motel, kindly drove me to the nearest hospital in the middle of the night. Very efficiently I was transferred onto a trolley, but not admitted into the hospital before I was able to prove to the receptionist that I was covered by Blue Cross. I still wonder what would have happened to me if I had not been covered. In all my time in the USA I cannot ever recall seeing a hospital with a sign "Free Treatment".

Average costs for treatment in the USA work out at £1,000 for a broken limb, and £25,000 for a heart attack. Just calling out an ambulance can cost you £1,500.

Where does one go if not covered by medical insurance? Perhaps it's best not to know, just make sure you are covered before you travel to the States. Incidentally, my one night in the US hospital cost $400, and that was fifteen years ago.

On the other hand, treatment in a Libyan hospital for three broken ribs cost me nothing. I was also treated like a patient, not a carcase of meat as was the case in the USA. Perhaps the colour of my card was wrong; maybe gold would have been better than blue.

If one has to fall sick there is no better place to do it than Saudi Arabia, with the possible exception of Switzerland. The hospitals that I visited in Dhahran were like something out of a science fiction film and the medical staff some of the best in the business. I am eternally grateful to them for the treatment I received when suffering from a very distressing virus that was attacking my eyes. At home in Devon I had been treated for wrongly diagnosed conjunctivitis for two weeks prior to returning from leave. I dread to think of the outcome if I had not been working in the Kingdom at that time.

I was working for ARAMCO at the time so all my treatment was free. I believe all medical treatment in Saudi Arabia is now free for foreign workers, but I am not so sure about visiting families. With the annual pilgrimage, or Haj, to Mecca, millions of people pour into the Kingdom from all over the globe. Outbreaks of cholera and typhoid are not unknown so make sure all necessary inoculations are up to date before visiting the country, or any other Muslim country at the time of the Haj.

Precautions

The most important thing to do before embarking on any foreign trip is to ensure you have taken all the necessary precautions, such as having all the relevant inoculations and commencing any anti-malaria treatment. As briefly mentioned in a previous chapter, your GP or local health centre will advise you as to what precautions are necessary. Most travel agents are also able to supply this information or, if you wish, you can access the web at *www.surgerydoor.co.uk* where the subject is well documented.

Many inoculations are available for free on the NHS from your local health centre. However, certain injections such as rabies, Japanese encephalitis, and yellow fever are not normally kept in stock and will have to be specially ordered and paid for.

There is also a helpline for travellers available from Medical Advisory Services for Travellers Abroad (MASTA). Expert advice is on offer from its extensive database validated by the London School of Hygiene and Tropical Medicine. The telephone number is 0891 224100.You can also call the Centre for Tropical Diseases at 020 7388 9600

One in a hundred travellers are reckoned to become seriously ill with one complaint or another (one in twenty-five in the Indian subcontinent), so it is worth taking every possible precaution. A recent survey showed that one in five people caught a cold after any flight over two hours, probably just due to the proximity of other passengers.

The rapid movement across the globe of the recent SARS virus, during which 800 people worldwide died, proved how easy contamination is spread by air travel. Short of giving every passenger a medical before flying I see no way of preventing this happening. I can recall times in the past when on an aircraft in an infected area, being informed that before take-off the interior, which included all passengers, would be sprayed to ensure no bugs would be carried to the next destination. Perhaps this procedure should be adapted at every stop.

One does not necessarily have to go to exotic places to contract some of the earth's nastiest diseases. Very recently bubonic plague, (the black death responsible for 50 million fatalities in the Middle Ages), was confirmed in a couple from New Mexico who were on vacation in New York. Owing to the heightened alert of possible terrorist attacks, New York hospitals had been warned this disease was a likely weapon and were therefore aware of it. The chances of it having been diagnosed so early back home in New Mexico are very unlikely. The operation to discover where the disease had originated was so successful the actual disease-bearing rat was found in the couple's garden. The flea that bit rat, husband, and wife is probably still on the FBI's Most Wanted list.

There are an average of 2,000 cases per year worldwide of bubonic plague of which 50% are normally fatal even when treated with powerful antibiotics. The disease is highly contagious and can be contracted by breathing the same air as an infected person. The symptoms are large sores filled with dark, rotting blood followed by pneumonia as the lungs begin to rot. Not very pleasant at all.

Another nasty complaint that can be contracted in the USA is West Nile virus. It was originally an African disease of birds but is now present in at least six American states extending from New York to Florida. It is spread by mosquitoes biting infected birds, mostly crows in the USA, then going on to bite humans. The effect on victims, both birds and humans, is a swelling of the brain and paralysis.

We are informed that smallpox has virtually been eradicated and the vaccination is no longer mandatory, but I keep mine up to date just as a precaution as I still see young people with pox scars whenever I visit certain parts of Africa.

In West Africa it is advisable to take precautions against all manner of nasty ailments; yellow fever, blackwater fever, malaria, bilharzia, and Lassa fever to name but a few. Simple common sense behaviour such as not bathing in rivers and not eating unwashed fruit can cut down the risks quite considerably. Be especially careful of salads wherever travelling overseas. It is not only British restaurants that fail to wash the lettuce properly.

The drinking water in Lagos was of a higher standard than that of London according to an article I once read in *Time* magazine, but it is still probably advisable to drink bottled water wherever one goes. Your stomach may not be able to cope with the minerals in the local water. Judging by the amount of Evian and Perrier you will see purchased by the indigenous population of whatever local supermarket you are in, the natives' stomachs have the same problem.

Although, of all the continents, Europe has probably the safest water, we are still the biggest consumers of bottled water on earth. Italy both bottles and consumes the most, around 6.5 billion litres per annum. Worldwide 35 billion litres are consumed each year – enough to fill 14,000 Olympic size swimming pools.

Remember that many hotels and bars do not use bottled water for the ice cubes they so liberally place into your drinks.

No matter where one travels, or how often, there is always the risk of stomach trouble. Known all over the world by such euphemisms as "Montezuma's Revenge", "Gyppy Tummy", "Back Door Trots", or simply "The Runs" it can be a simple touch of gastroenteritis or the sign of something more serious such as dysentery or typhoid. It is advisable to carry one of the many available medicines in case of trouble and to seek medical advice if the symptoms persist. I have always found *Imodium* ideal for run of the mill stomach upsets.

A recent league published by a travel agency listed the following as the places where one was most likely to suffer stomach trouble; Egypt, Kenya, Dominican Republic, Mexico, Tunisia, Greece, and the West Indies. I spent six months in the Sinai, Egypt in 1993 and have visited the country on many other occasions without ever suffering from stomach problems. I have also been in and out of Tunisia and Kenya on many occasions without any trouble. The only place I have ever been hospitalised for food poisoning was in the USA, so it seems to me one can take the so called league tables with a pinch of salt. It all boils down to taking the basic precautions, and a lot of luck. Incidentally, there are one hundred cases of food poisoning reported in the UK annually.

Travellers to West African countries such as The Gambia, Ghana, Sierra Leone, and Nigeria should be very wary of the tumbla fly. This insect likes to lay its eggs in damp washing which many Africans lay out on the bushes to dry in the sun. Your hotel laundry could well be guilty of this act as washing lines are by no means a common feature in Africa.

The eggs hatch when in contact with a warm human body, which can be on bed sheets or in articles of clothing. The emerging maggot is so tiny it easily burrows under the skin of whoever has been unfortunate enough to hatch it, without the victim being aware of it until some days later when it starts to grow. The result is a large, painful, boil that grows to accommodate the creature inside. If left, the maggot will develop into a full grown tumbla fly before emerging, but the normal treatment is to cover the swelling with a thick layer of Vaseline which cuts off the insect's air supply and forces it to emerge before it is fully developed.

I have seen local children in Nigeria with as many as six of these creatures at one time on various parts of the body. Never leave damp swimwear hanging over the veranda rails and press all washing with a very hot iron to destroy any eggs that are laid. Following these simple precautions my wife and children lived for two years in West Africa without any tumbla fly problems. I believe this creature, or something very similar, is also known as the bott fly in some parts of Central and South America.

Other flying insects to be aware of are bees and hornets. Fortunately, most people already have a healthy regard for these creatures as I expect most of us have been stung sometime in our lives, in more ways than one! However, some overseas varieties of the bee family are far deadlier than those encountered on a holiday picnic back home. Owing to man messing with nature (again), the killer bee of South America is now common in most southern states of the USA. This bee was produced by some idiot in Brazil in the fifties crossing the mild tempered European honeybee with its rather bad tempered African cousin. Surprise, surprise, the resultant strain had all the bad characteristics of the African bee.

There have already been many recorded deaths in the States due to these creatures, the first in 1991. In Mexico the total recently hit 400. The bees will attack anyone who approaches too close to their nests. They also colonise at ten times the rate of a normal honeybee. At the last observation they were spreading north at the rate of two hundred miles per year. Canada, here we come!

The killer bees, or *Africanised bees,* as they are more popularly known, are aggravated by vibrations from machinery such as lawn mowers and chain saws that they regard as some kind of threat to their environment. (They have my sympathy here.) However, unlike most of us, they do not go inside or close the windows, they get angry and prepare to defend themselves. Their venom is no stronger than that of the honeybee, it is the sheer number of stings that causes death. Five hundred stings is the equivalent of a rattlesnake bite.

Contrary to popular belief, they do not immediately intend to kill their victim. Research in Mexico has shown that their initial attack, much like that of the elephant, is a warning. They actually fly into their victims without stinging on the first foray. Bees are intelligent creatures, they realise the act of stinging means certain death. It is only if the intruder acts aggressively, continuing to approach the nest or hitting them with flailing arms that they go into attack mode. They are prepared to die for their cause.

So, if you are unlucky enough to intrude into a killer bee's territory, cover your face with your hands, keep calm, turn around, and retrace your steps. Much easier said than done I would believe.

One magazine I read recently was advising readers wanting to travel to exotic places to arm themselves with a roll of masking tape to block off any vents giving access to flying insects. I fear this could cause even more severe problems with fumes from water heaters that are notoriously unsafe in many overseas countries. Make do with an insect repellent and a can of Scram or Raid.

If you are concerned about being stung you may consider purchasing a French invention, the *Aspivenin*. The device looks like a syringe with a cup-shaped nozzle in place of the needle. If you are bitten you simply pull the plunger, place the nozzle over the bite and then push the plunger back in. The resultant vacuum (ten times more powerful than you can suck) draws the poison out. You need to hold it for twenty to thirty seconds for a mosquito bite, ninety seconds for a bee or wasp sting. The device also works for spiders, scorpions, and snakes, but I for one would not like to test it on the bite of a black mamba or pit viper.

For minor insect bites and cuts I have found tea tree oil quite effective.

Never run about anywhere overseas in bare feet. There are other tiny creatures similar to the tumbla fly that are waiting for a host, and bare feet are an open invitation to them. Besides the invisible menace there are also spiders, scorpions, and similar nasties lurking in the undergrowth. Many people are unaware that poisonous spiders are also present in the UK. The woodlouse spider is one, but, as its name suggests, it is more interested in biting woodlice than humans. Also, its bite is not fatal to humans, unlike the funnel web spider of Australia, the wolf spider of Asia, and the black widow spider of the United States, to name but a few.

The black widow spider in the USA has venom fifteen times more toxic than a rattlesnake, and bites around five thousand people annually. Owing to the fact that it injects only a tiny amount, and because antivenom is usually readily available, very few bites prove to be fatal, but they are extremely painful.

A brief read of any American hunting, shooting, and fishing magazine will enlighten any would-be hikers to the delights that await them in the mountains and forests. In the USA every year many people are bitten by snakes and spiders and attacked by a variety of bears. These include the grizzly and black bear, and the polar bear in Alaska. Black bears have taken to foraging for food in suburban areas as the towns have encroached into the mountains and forests. They are now considered pests on the outskirts of Los Angeles and at Mammoth Lakes in California. In Yosemite National Park they annually cause half a million dollars worth of damage to cars, trailers, tents, etc. Also known to inflict damage on wayward walkers are the moose, bison, and the mountain lion.

When it comes to danger from our feathered friends most of us think the greatest risk is choking on a chicken bone. However, in Africa there are many recorded cases of ostriches kicking people to death, and yet there are those amongst us daft enough to believe riding these creatures is fun.

I briefly mentioned not bathing in African rivers in an earlier paragraph. Besides the risk of disease, especially bilharzia (or liver fluke as it is usually referred to), there is also the risk of being grabbed by the odd crocodile or hippopotamus.

Hippos, often the model for cuddly toys, may look harmless as they laze about in the rivers, but actually are responsible for more deaths on the African continent than snakes. They can be thoroughly bad-tempered and upturn boats just for the hell of it. A male hippo can weigh four tons and though an herbivore, has huge teeth that can sever a crocodile. The crocodile, incidentally, kills around 400 people every year.

While working at Kasane Airport, Botswana, I often took a boat trip along the Chobe River into the game reserve. This was the place immortalized to thousands of Americans by Richard Burton and Elizabeth Taylor deciding to hold one of their marriages there. The reserve abounds with elephants, hippos, baboons, giraffes, buffalo, and a great variety of antelope. There are also lions and rhinos but these are harder to find.

No matter how often I went onto the river I never quite became accustomed to hippos suddenly popping up a few feet from the boat, usually with a roar and tremendous splash. Just days before I had arrived a local fisherman had been attacked in his canoe. He was seen to dive into the water but never surfaced. Experienced hunters told me he was probably bitten under water by a mother hippo protecting her calf. The massive wounds inflicted by the bite would have meant his body no longer being able to float to the surface and would have been devoured by crocodiles in no time at all.

It is not only while swimming in rivers overseas that one is at risk, the sea can be equally dangerous. The Caribbean, the Red Sea, the Persian (or Arabian) Gulf, the Indian Ocean, in fact, all tropical seas contain any number of living organisms waiting to bite, sting, or poison the unwary bather.

Besides the obvious dangers from sharks and barracuda, there are also sea snakes to whose poison there is no known antidote. There are also poison corals, sea urchins, sea cucumbers, jellyfish, and stonefish all of which can curtail a business trip or holiday, or even a life. The beautiful cone shells of the Indo-Pacific seas also contain a poison strong enough to kill. More fanciful creatures such as the octopus, giant clam, and huge squid are also lurking in the deep. Incidentally, the blue ringed octopus of Australia is reputed to be, pound for pound, the deadliest creature on the planet. Although only about eight inches (20 cms) across its tentacles it carries enough venom to kill ten adults.

Another Australian creature to avoid is the irukandji, a tiny jellyfish the size of an acorn. Its half metre long tentacles contain a deadly poison that causes intense pain, cramp, and nausea. A lot of deaths previously attributed to heart attacks and accidental drowning are believed now to have been caused by brushes with this little horror. There is now a current boom in jellyfish numbers of all kinds owing to the warming of the oceans and fertilizer runoff on which they feed. Other nasties awaiting the unwary in Australia include the porcupine fish, lionfish, the box jellyfish, (or *chironex,* whose venom kills far more quickly than a cobra*),* and even the quaint looking duck-billed platypus has a venomous claw. On the subject of venom, Australia has eleven of the world's most poisonous snakes on land and thirty sea snakes including one whose venom is twenty times more deadly than a cobra's. Fancy a stroll in the outback or a dip in the ocean?

While sailing off the coast of Oman a colleague of mine slipped over the side of the boat to tie up alongside the jetty at Salalah. The water was clear and only a metre deep so he omitted to replace his protective footwear. He stepped directly onto a stingray that had buried itself in the sand. The injury to his foot was horrendous, and days later the stench of the rotting flesh on his foot was overpowering as we entered his hospital room. It was weeks before he left hospital with a large part of his foot now missing.

The lure of the blue ocean is irresistible in the tropics, but be warned, and be careful. It should also not be forgotten that it is not only overseas that bathers should beware. In my own home county of Devon only last year a woman was hospitalised for five days after being stung by a jellyfish while wading waist deep in the sea off the Westward Ho! coast, and many bathers had to be treated for cuts to the feet after stepping on razor shells at Torbay.

When I first arrived in West Africa I was horrified by the amount of snakes to be found there and hardly a day passed by without a green mamba, a cobra, or a king sized python appearing somewhere. Fortunately for me, the company's agent had lived in Africa for forty years and was able to reassure me that snakes were as eager to avoid me as I was to avoid them.

His advice when working in the bush was to always wear a sturdy pair of boots, preferably a pair that covered the ankles, and to also make a lot of noise when walking through the undergrowth. Many people are bitten by snakes that they have either trodden on, or surprised while the creatures were warming themselves in the sun. Snakes do not have ears but they can feel the slightest vibrations and will get out of your way if they sense you are approaching.

I have heard some ridiculous notions where snakes are concerned, including the supposed fact that a python cannot crush a man if he is on open ground as it needs a tree or root to anchor itself to in order to be able to coil. The truth is, it will wrap its tail around the victim's leg and tighten from there.

I have also heard that snuff is lethal to a snake. This may very well be, but how the Hell do you get the creature to take the stuff? My advice is if you do come across a snake don't waste time trying to determine whether or not it is a poisonous variety, assume it is and retreat rapidly.

Beware of dogs everywhere abroad as the UK is one of the very few areas that is still completely free of rabies. In Africa and the Middle East give all dogs a wide berth. Over the past ten years the disease has rapidly spread westwards across Europe and is now to be found just across the Channel. I expect with the existence of the Channel Tunnel there is the possibility that rats, mice, or other creatures, probably bats, will bring the disease to Britain.

At one time, while serving in the Royal Air Force overseas, there was always a plentiful supply of salt tablets on the table at every meal to which we dutifully helped ourselves. Like the X-ray machines in shoe shops, these were suddenly and silently withdrawn. They were evidently no longer considered beneficial, or alternatively, like the X-ray machines, considered downright dangerous. In Russia all microwave ovens are now considered to be dangerous and the public warned against using them. Can we expect the west to follow this example in the near future? I think not, too many multinational companies involved. Anyway, salt tablets are certainly not required if one is healthy and eating a balanced diet, no matter how hot it gets.

The taking of anti-malaria medication is recommended for most tropical countries. No matter how liberally you smother yourself with insect repellent you are going to suffer the occasional mosquito bite. If it happens to be from the female *anopheles* mosquito then the chances are it is carrying the malaria parasite. More people die from contact with the mosquito than any other creature on earth. The World Health Organisation estimates that malaria kills a million people each year, with 300-500 million being infected. Even if you recover from malaria you can be fairly sure that you will suffer further bouts throughout your remaining years and could possibly sustain permanent damage to the brain, liver, or spleen. Therefore, the taking of anti-malaria medication is essential when visiting tropical zones. There are various brands to choose from, some daily tablets and some weekly ones that are known as "Sunday-Sunday" medicine in Nigeria. All anti-malaria treatment should be commenced at least one week before departure and continued for two weeks after return from your trip.

There is a new anti-malarial drug on the market, Malarone, which is reported to have negligible side effects. One need only take it one or two days before arriving in an infected area and for seven days after leaving. I have not used it myself so cannot vouch for it. Studies have shown that it prevents malaria in more than 95% of cases. If that is true, then it is well worth considering.

For reasons unknown to science the local inhabitants of Papua New Guinea are immune to malaria. When the gene that protects them is isolated it may be possible that the rest of us will be offered immunity, at a price! In the meantime, keep taking the tablets.

It is also possible to purchase mosquito nets impregnated with the insecticide *Permethrin*. Some time ago the World Health Organisation supported trials on these nets on children between one and four in West Africa with very good results. The big problem I found using mosquito nets was that no matter how carefully I tucked everything in, by the morning there were gaps everywhere and I was bitten horribly. In hotels my usual routine was to check the windows were shut, pull the curtains across, give the room a thorough good squirting of Shelltox or something similar, then adjourn to the bar. Hopefully, by the time I returned the room was clear of fumes and insects.

Owing to the developed nations that no longer have malaria, pressurising the nations that still do to give up the use of DDT, malaria cases are now rising at a rate of 20% per annum in many parts of the world. Everyone agrees that a ton of DDT used to fumigate a cotton field is unacceptable, but surely two grams per square metre to treat the inside of houses to prevent thousands of deaths is not too much to ask? Once again it is the over-zealous environmentalists who are to blame demanding a total ban instead of a controlled use of the chemical.

The mosquito is also responsible for carrying the Rift Valley Fever virus. Although nowhere nearly as prevalent as malaria, this rather unpleasant disease killed over 400 victims in Kenya and Somalia during an outbreak in 1998. It was originally identified as a disease of sheep and cattle in the thirties but in the seventies it made the transition to humans. The virus liquefies the brain and other major organs and the victim then haemorrhages from every orifice.

I once heard that the definition of intimidation was one mosquito in a dark bedroom.

If taking medication regularly in the UK, or anywhere else if it comes to that, it is advisable to have a word with your GP before proceeding abroad. Drugs such as tetracycline can sensitise the skin to ultra-violet radiation. Acne sufferers on this drug should enquire about the possibility of switching to erthromycin while holidaying abroad. Tranquillisers such as the phenothiazine group can also cause serious skin problems.

A word of warning here; be careful if forced to purchase medicines overseas. Check with Customs on your return because there are substances sold abroad for medicinal purposes that are illegal here because of certain ingredients they contain. Obviously, it would be irresponsible of me to list such medicines here.

Many people are turning to herbal remedies for use when travelling. Homeopaths recommend echinacea and acidophilus to boost the immune system's ability to combat unfamiliar germs. For advice contact the British Homeopathic Association on 020 7935 2163.

One bit of good news is that some airlines now operate a "telemedicine" link whereby trained staff on board the aircraft can communicate with a doctor on the ground in case of an emergency. Vital signs such as blood pressure, pulse, and temperature are relayed via sensors so that treatment can commence immediately a person is taken ill. The doctor can then make the decision whether or not to divert the aeroplane.

If taken ill overseas beware of local cures. When I suffered a broken leg in Port Harcourt my driver offered to take me to his village to see the local witch doctor. I declined the offer even though my driver insisted he had been treated for a similar injury with a bandage of banana leaves and within two weeks could carry a bag of cement above his head. Even before I broke my leg I doubt if I could have matched that feat.

In the Far East all manner of cure-alls are available. Locals swear by snake's blood and ground tiger bones, but the occasional Ginseng tablet is all I ventured to take. I do object most strongly to magnificent animals like the tiger and rhinoceros being slaughtered so that some oriental hypochondriac can consume some peculiar part of its anatomy.

In an emergency I once had occasion to consult a Pakistani doctor after I had managed to stand on a camel thorn which penetrated my boot and imbedded itself in the sole of my left foot. The thorn had been removed but my foot was swollen and throbbed painfully. The doctor, who I confess had a good reputation, examined the wound.

"Fomentation" he said after deliberating for a short while.

"I beg your pardon?" I replied.

"Fomentation."

"Oh, is it?" I enquired.

"No, no. Fomentation is the treatment" came the reply.

"What is fomentation?" I asked patiently.

"It is an English word" he retorted.

"It may very well be, doctor" I said, "but I am an engineer not a physician."

"It is a very common English word!" he persisted.

I eventually persuaded him to explain to me what fomentation meant. He said I should find a large, smooth stone, put it into the fire until it was hot then place my aching foot on it. He assured me that this action was guaranteed to stop the pain. I am afraid my faith in fomentation was not as strong as his, so, in considerable pain I drove miles into the mountains to where Marconi were installing a microwave link, and there their resident nurse was good enough to give me a course of penicillin injections and some much needed painkillers.

The problem of AIDS and to a lesser extent, hepatitis, means one has to be extremely careful if needing a blood transfusion overseas. I am certain any half decent insurance company would insist on a patient returning to the UK, if at all possible, for any surgery required. Carrying a couple of pints of spare blood abroad is a bit extreme, but not unknown, but for anyone going overseas for an extended period it is well worthwhile taking a compact First Aid kit with a sterilised hypodermic syringe.

On the subject of needles and with the present craze of festooning the body with any chunk of metal that comes to hand, I think it prudent to mention that puncturing any part of the human torso is an open invitation for stray bugs or bacteria to enter. I know hundreds of thousands of British sailors have been tattooed safely for centuries, but that was before AIDS and hepatitis were as prevalent as they now are. Being tattooed or pierced while overseas is asking for trouble. Four out of every five cases of HIV infection reported in the UK result from moments of indiscretion abroad.

Returning to the subject of AIDS, or Acquired Immune Deficiency Syndrome, I once heard three eminent medical men arguing very heatedly on the origins of the disease, if disease it is.

I was having dinner alone in a hotel in Uganda in August 1991 when I heard a heated discussion going on at a nearby table. I am not normally a nosey person but as they were talking quite loudly I could not help but overhear. Two of the men present, who I later discovered were British and Danish medical experts, were accusing the other, an American, of belonging to the country that deliberately manufactured the virus responsible for the epidemic that then, as now, was running rife in Africa.

Their arguments to me seemed most plausible. They claimed the virus had been manufactured as part of a chemical weapons programme by American laboratories. The virus had been tested on long-term prison inmates who, with seemingly no chance of release, were quite happy to earn money in this way to buy luxuries such as TVs and drugs. With the prisoners serving sentences as long as 999 years with no chance of parole the scientists were content that their guinea pigs would be around until the end of the experiments.

Unfortunately, someone in authority (President Jimmy Carter?), suddenly decided that, "no man should live without hope". The fact that the inmates were rioting (fifty killed in New Mexico in February 1980), and murdering prison guards with impunity may have had something to do with it. Having abolished the death penalty in many states there was no punishment worse than the one already imposed upon the inmates that they could be threatened with. The promise of possible parole was intended to quell the riots.

The consequence was that several long-term prisoners who never expected to be released were suddenly set free, including one or two on the programme.

One can only imagine the panic that then ensued. There was no way the scientists could admit what they had been doing. The prisoners were released into the community. Naturally they would head for the big cities where no questions are asked of strangers and where they could get lost among the crowds.

Having spent twenty to thirty years with no female company it was inevitable that they would have developed homosexual tendencies, which neatly explains why the disease swept through the gay populations of New York and San Francisco in December 1981.

Having no modern skills, even trying to drive after twenty years off the road would have been impossible, the only jobs available were unskilled labour such as deckhands and stevedores. Ships regularly sail from ports on the east and west coasts of America to places all around the world. No great surprise then that the next big flare-up of the AIDS virus was in African coastal regions where bars and brothels compete for customers. Within three years the virus was in 150 different countries.

In the bar of the hotel later I discovered that there were experts from many parts of the globe in Uganda at the time for a seminar in Kampala to discuss the growing AIDS problem. I have no way of knowing if what I heard that evening bears any relation to the truth. My two fellow diners may have been just winding up their US companion for all I know. If so, they certainly succeeded.

Diseases
I think here might be a good time to give a brief summary of some of the diseases one is likely to come in contact with when travelling abroad.

Cholera
When I was in the services it was compulsory to have an injection against this disease every year, but the last time I applied at my local health centre I was informed that the vaccine is no longer available in the UK. This surprised me as it is a highly infectious disease and outbreaks certainly do occur from time to time in tropical regions. I recall a very serious outbreak in the eighties that occurred at the time of the annual pilgrimage to Mecca (the *Haj*), when hundreds of people died as the disease was spread from Saudi Arabia to almost every other Muslim country. In 1988 a summer outbreak in New Delhi, India, affected thousands of residents and resulted in a death toll of over 200 even with modern medication.

Danger areas for this disease include Africa, South America, and South East Asia. Symptoms show one to three days after infection when there is vomiting and watery diarrhoea. Dehydration usually occurs due to high fluid loss. The disease can be fatal in as little as twenty-four hours if not treated. It is generally transmitted by contaminated liquid and foods that have been infected by a sufferer or carrier of the disease. Another good reason to be extremely careful when eating food prepared by someone else.

Hepatitis A

This is a virus that again is found in unclean food, especially seafood, and water. It causes inflammation of the liver and is very infectious. It is prevalent everywhere outside of Western Europe, North America, Australia, and New Zealand. An anti-hepatitis injection is available and should be administered four weeks before travel.

Hepatitis B

This is a worldwide virus spread by intimate person-to-person contact. It is spread by exactly the same means as the AIDS virus; having sex with an infected person, sharing contaminated needles, or transfusions with contaminated blood. There is a vaccine available but the course of treatment takes six months so is not really practical for the holiday traveller. It is definitely recommended for the itinerant voyager.

There is an alternative vaccine available which, although only giving 80% coverage against the disease, has the advantage of being an accelerated treatment. Your local health centre should be able to advise on this.

Typhoid

This disease again is found in contaminated food and water and is widespread in places with poor sanitation such as much of the Indian subcontinent. Typhoid is caused by the *salmonella typhi* organism and the symptoms include severe headache, red spots on the abdomen and chest, fever, and constipation which later turns to diarrhoea. There is a vaccine available that gives protection for three years, and this should be administered two weeks before travel.

Malaria

This disease, which is spread by the bite of the female mosquito, occurs in most tropical regions including Central Africa, South and Central America, and the Far East. It kills over a million people worldwide every year so it is essential to take precautions if visiting an affected area. There are various strains of malaria, the most lethal being cerebral malaria. As mentioned earlier in the chapter, anti-malarial precautions should commence before travelling (read instructions for whatever medication being used) and continued after return to the UK. Symptoms, which may take up to ten months to appear, are recurrent fevers causing alternate sweating and shivering. Avoid stagnant water and take precautions to prevent attack by mosquitoes, i.e. use an insect repellent. I found a liberal dose of aftershave discouraged the insects but, judging by the way my wife was bitten, perfume had the opposite effect!

In 1947 an epidemic of malaria affected 75 million people in India. An estimated one million died from the disease.

Japanese Encephalitis

Like malaria this disease is also transmitted by a mosquito bite. It is a viral disease that causes serious inflammation of the brain, can lead to permanent brain damage, and has a high mortality rate. Fortunately, in the majority of cases it only produces a mild, flu-like illness with no effect on the brain.

The disease is prevalent in large areas of Asia including China, Sri Lanka, the Philippines, Nepal, Indonesia, and Japan, but is fairly uncommon in tourists and short-term visitors.

When the virus enters the victim's bloodstream via the mosquito's saliva, it replicates itself in a variety of cells including those of the central nervous system causing the symptoms to appear.

There are similar flaviviruses, the family to which this virus belongs, which include, St Louis flavivirus in southern USA; Murray Valley flavivirus in Australia and Russian Spring Summer flavivirus. Other varieties, including Venezuelan equine encephalitis can be found in South America.

There is a vaccine available that is recommended if you intend to spend more than three weeks in an infected area.

Yellow Fever

Another disease spread by mosquito bites and is found mostly in Central America and West Africa. However, in August-September 1878, yellow fever claimed 5,000 victims in Memphis, Tennessee, before spreading south and claiming 4,000 in New Orleans and a further 2,000 in Greenville, Mississippi.

It attacks the liver and kidneys and was responsible for West Africa becoming known as "the white man's grave". There is a vaccine available which lasts ten years but this can only be obtained at a WHO Yellow Fever Centre and is not available free on the NHS. Symptoms are similar to those of malaria.

Rabies

As everyone knows this disease can be transmitted by the bite from a rabid dog, but is everyone aware that the saliva of *any* infected animal can pass on the virus? With the exception of the UK, Australia, and New Zealand, no country, not even the USA, is safe from this very distressing disease. Symptoms, in the early stages, include fever, headaches, stiff neck, anxiety, and disorientation. Later stages include an irrational fear of water, madness, and death.

There is a vaccine available that consists of a long course of injections, so, unless you are off to work in the local zoo, precaution when dealing with animals overseas is probably the best course of action.

Poliomyelitis
More commonly referred to as polio this infectious viral disease affects the central nervous system and can cause temporary or permanent paralysis and death. It is found everywhere outside the developed world, and occasionally inside it.

In the summer of 1946 this crippling disease struck down more than 25,000 victims, most of them children, in twenty-three states of the USA. It was the last major polio epidemic before the introduction of effective vaccines.

Like many other diseases it is spread by water and contaminated food. Vaccination is by way of oral drops and treatment should start at least three months before travelling if being vaccinated for the first time. A booster is available for previously vaccinated persons.

Diphtheria
This highly infectious disease, now rare in the UK and other developed countries, is still common in Eastern Europe and Russia. It causes obstruction of the upper air passages and causes death by asphyxiation. It is spread by contact with an infected person. A course of injections is recommended for anyone expecting to spend time in an infected area. Most UK residents born after 1940 will have been immunised in childhood but should consider utilising the low-dose vaccine that is now available.

Meningitis
Recent outbreaks in the UK have reminded people that this dangerous disease is still a serious threat. There are various forms of meningitis transmitted either by viruses or bacteria. Types A and C can be protected against by injections. Symptoms are fever, sore throat, headache, and sometimes a rash. Places where the disease is a problem include South Africa, Saudi Arabia, and India.

Tetanus

This bacterial disease is found worldwide and anyone working in agriculture or the building industry should already be regularly injected against it. However, it is common practice to be injected against it on admission to casualty with any open wound.

Allow three months before travel if being inoculated for the first time. The disease, which is also known as "lockjaw", causes muscle spasms in the face and neck. Early symptoms are a sore throat and headache.

Tuberculosis

This disease is to be found in Africa, Asia, Central and South America, and also in Eastern Europe. However, precautions need only be taken by persons expecting to stay a month or more in these areas, and who also expect to come into close contact with the local community.

The WHO sees tuberculosis as the planet's most urgent health problem and the UK is seeing an increasing return of this disease once thought to have been eradicated for ever from these shores.

A third of all patients with the HIV virus die of tuberculosis.

Thankfully the worst diseases are also the most rare, but certainly not unknown to the modern tourist. Six of the nastiest are as follows.

Anthrax

This is considered to be the most likely germ to be utilised in the event of a terrorist attack. It is particularly nasty as it comes in three varieties; cutaneous, inhalation, and gastrointestinal. It commences with flu-like symptoms and ends with the lungs flooding and drowning the patient in his own bodily fluids. Antibiotics are a possible cure but the death rate is still 75%.

Ebola

The most lethal disease known to man but thankfully, as far as I am aware, confined to a small part of Africa. It is caused by filovirus germs attacking living tissue so that the whole body – muscles, organs, and membranes – disintegrate. Blood is emitted from every orifice until the body is drained. There is no known effective treatment and fatalities are 90 – 100%.

Lassa Fever

Another of Africa's delights, this virus kills around 5,000 people a year. Symptoms are high fever, vomiting, diarrhoea, nosebleeds, and internal bleeding leading to fluid on the lungs and fits from a swollen brain. Can be treated if caught in time with an anti-viral drug such as Ribavirin. Death results in around 20% of cases.

Necrotising Fascitis
There is no need to travel overseas to find this particular horror. Cases of this flesh eating disease have occurred many times in the UK and the USA in recent years. It is caused by a mutation of streptococcus, the everyday sore throat bug. In just hours it can eat through skin and commence dissolving the membrane between muscles and soft tissue. Drastic treatment involves cutting away large areas of infected skin, plus antibiotics. Usually 40% fatal, but patients who do recover can be hideously scarred.

Smallpox
Not considered worth vaccinating against anymore but I always keep my injections up to date as mentioned earlier. Pimples grow into huge, pus-filled blisters. Large sections of unattached skin can then just slide off. Patients can die of shock or bleed to death. There is no known treatment and the chance of death is around 30%.

Medical treatment should be sought immediately symptoms of any disease appear, but, should you find yourself in a position where no professional help is immediately available remember that dehydration is the main danger where stomach problems are involved. A useful rehydration mixture is as follows.

Four teaspoons of sugar, half a teaspoon of salt, a pint of boiled water, and half a pint of orange juice (any fruit juice if orange not available). This is a good drink for replacing body fluids when suffering from any kind of diarrhoea.

Economy Class Syndrome
A lot of publicity has lately been given to Economy Class Syndrome, or Deep Vein Thrombosis to give it its medical term. I must have flown the best part of a million miles in the last fifty years without any problems at all. It, therefore, surprises me that now, when aircraft are far roomier and luxurious than they were when I commenced flying that this problem is now occurring. I am inclined to think that it is the fault of the passenger and not the aircraft. How come we never hear of a member of the Armed Forces, especially the Royal Air Force, suffering from this condition? The fact that they are fit and healthy may have something to do with it.

DVT is part of a condition known as Venous Thrombo-Embolism, the other part being PE, or Pulmonary Embolism. VTE simply means blood clots in the veins that get into the blood stream. The three main causes of Deep Vein Thrombosis are, changes in blood flow, changes in blood constituents, changes in the vein wall.

Blood Flow

This is obviously affected by posture. How many of us wake up in the morning with a dead arm or leg, or pins and needles in the fingers? When flying long distances it is advisable to wiggle your toes and feet occasionally and, if convenient get up and move about.

Blood Constituents

Genetic factors of the blood cannot be changed. If you are born with a tendency to form clots in your veins (thrombophilia), as 30% of the population are, then you are obviously at more risk. A blood test can determine this if you are concerned.

Factors that can be changed are those caused by dehydration, oestrogen levels, varicose veins, and smoking.

To avoid dehydration when flying drink plenty of water and fruit juice, normally supplied free, but cut down on tea, coffee, and alcohol.

The oral contraceptive pill is known to increase the risk of DVT. The jury is still out regarding the affects of HRT. The decision is yours as to whether or not you continue taking the medication.

Varicose veins cause a pump failure of the legs and constricted blood flow. This causes clots in the varicose veins (superficial thrombophlebitis), or in the deep veins (DVT). If you suffer from varicose veins you take a risk every time you fly.

Smoking activates the platelets and damages the vein walls thus increasing the risk of clots in the arteries. The airlines are doing us all a favour by banning smoking on all flights.

Vein Walls

Vein walls are affected by local pressures on the legs. There are a variety of support stockings and socks available for both men and women if you feel you need them.

Aspirin has been recommended by some of the medical profession as it thins the blood by preventing platelets in the blood from working, but it can cause stomach problems and most experts agree it does nothing to prevent DVT. The best advice is drink plenty of water and fruit juice, exercise when possible, and if you are not fit don't fly!

It is worth remembering that wherever you go in search of better weather the sun is probably going to be a lot brighter than that to which you are accustomed. Sunshine contains a mixture of light frequencies including ultraviolet rays (UVA and UVB), and the more hazardous longer wave blue light. These can cause damage to the cornea and the lens of the eyes leading to cataracts in the long term. I speak from experience having had cataracts removed from both eyes at a relatively young age. Sunglasses, therefore, are a prerequisite for overseas travel. Ensure those purchased have the British Standard number 2724:1987 or are guaranteed to give protection from invisible UV light.

It is also a good idea to carry a spare pair of spectacles with you if you have them, failing that, a copy of your prescription will ensure you can get a replacement pair should you need them. People with false teeth are also advised to carry a spare set; even old dentures are preferable to none at all. We have all heard stories of seasick passengers who have lost more than their last meal over the ship's side.

Many years ago I had occasion to share a dining room with a family from Clerkenwell in London. Old Granny, much to the disgust of her grandchildren, would remove her dentures and wrap them in the napkin before every meal. When one of them plucked up enough courage to remonstrate with her she replied, "I can't eat wiv 'em. They're only for smiling wiv."

I shared her son's feelings when he muttered under his breath, "Gor blimey, they're gonna last for ever!"

While on the subject of teeth, it is worthwhile having a dental check before travelling to far-flung places. I once had occasion to visit a Russian dentist for an emergency filling and, on my return to the UK, had the devil of a job trying to convince my dentist that it was not a DIY job carried out with building cement. If you wish to avoid emergency treatment while abroad you may consider investing £10.99 on the purchase of a "Dentanurse" kit from the local Boots chemists before travelling. It comprises of a mirror, some basic instruments, and a filling compound which will suffice for most minor tooth problems until you get back to see your own dentist.

Finally, a quick word about protection from the sun. I realise that the prime reason for travelling overseas is to guarantee that one does at least see the sun for a couple of weeks, but to lie in it until one becomes the colour of a kipper is the height of folly. In Australia they now have "beach police" who warn anyone they believe is over-exposing themselves to the sun's rays. The Civil Liberties brigade would probably be up in arms if anything similar was attempted in Britain. If you are tempted to lie in the sun at least use some form of barrier cream to cut out some of the harmful effects of ultraviolet rays.

Swimming pools in many continental resorts are "potentially lethal" according to a report by the Royal Society for the Prevention of Accidents. Sixty per cent of Britain's spinal injuries are sustained in swimming pools abroad. Poor water clarity, diving boards with an insufficient depth of water, and lack of pool markings are common faults in continental pools.

Another danger to be aware of overseas is "killer litter". In Venice the canals are used as garbage disposals by many of the inhabitants. I have had vegetable peelings cascade around me while enjoying a trip in a gondola. Dead pets often float by as well. Although this is most unpleasant it is not as dangerous as Singapore. There, television sets are often thrown from high-rise apartments. Around fifty people per year are arrested in Singapore on suspicion of throwing killer litter.

In Rome they have the peculiar custom of throwing something out of the window on New Year's Eve. It is their quaint way of saying down with the old. So, unless it is unavoidable, I suggest finding somewhere else to celebrate the arrival of the New Year.

The only time something similar happened to me in the UK was some years ago in Ilfracombe, Devon, when a complete Sunday lunch came crashing down into the road from an upstairs window of a house, missing me by only a couple of metres. I didn't hang around for the dessert.

If sensible precautions are taken the chances of contracting anything serious overseas are pretty remote. However, there is one thing that most people will suffer from and that is jet lag. It is most likely to affect those over thirty who are used to following an established daily routine. The effects of flying thousands of miles to the east or west cannot be completely eradicated but there are simple measures one can take to ease the problem. If flying east, try going to bed earlier than usual for a few nights before departure. If flying west, try staying up later than usual for a few nights before flying. High dose antioxidants such as vitamins C and E should be taken before, during and after flying, and plenty of fluids (not alcohol!) should be consumed throughout the flight.

I've always found that it only takes a day or so for the effects to wear off so have usually just got on with things.

Crime overseas

It is an unfortunate fact of life that no matter where one travels to, and irrespective of how idyllic the surroundings, crime is never too far away. Whether it is petty thievery by hotel staff, thankfully quite rare, or organised armed robbery as was rife in Nigeria in the late seventies. In Spain around 4,000 replacement passports are issued to British tourists every year, and hundreds are issued in Portugal and Holland. Some of these have just been lost but the vast majority stolen. Not too long ago, 10% of all British tourists visiting Bulgaria fell foul of thieves.

There should be no need for me to remind anyone to be on one's guard against crime when travelling. One should exercise just as much care in a tropical paradise as in a big city, probably more so, as a policeman is hardly likely to be around the corner. I shall, therefore, waste no time or space warning one of purse snatchers in Europe, muggers in the USA, or pickpockets everywhere. Although be wary of bag snatchers on scooters or motorbikes; they don't care too much if they happen to drag the owner along with the purse.

Be very suspicious if some Good Samaritan points out that you have some noxious substance on your coat or jacket. It is quite possible he/she has just squirted it there in order to be able to rifle your pockets while helping to clean up the mess.

Be extra vigilant in crowded places such as train and bus stations especially if the locals are eager to assist you with the purchase of tickets. While one is confusing you with questions like whether or not you require *"aller et retour"*, another will be picking your pocket.

On the subject of pickpockets, tourists should be extra wary in Jakarta, Indonesia. The problem there is so serious that the local authorities are planning to deter pickpockets by placing snipers on the rooftops with orders to shoot to kill any local thief going about his illegal business. A spokesman recently stated "We are confident they will be able to shoot thieves, rascals, and pickpockets without making too many mistakes". That's comforting!

Simple precautions like using travellers' cheques instead of cash will safeguard one's money, but be prepared to shop around to get the best rate of exchange. Banks will usually give a better rate than can be obtained at the hotel. In countries where they are to be found the FOREX is advisable or any *bureau de change.*

If changing large amounts of travellers' cheques for cash be as discreet as possible, and do not do it alone if it can be avoided. Also be extra careful when withdrawing from a cash machine. I have jumped back into the car and driven to a different machine on a few occasions when not happy with the unsavoury characters hanging around in nearby shop doorways; and that has not always been overseas.

Never give bank account details to anyone and check closely all plastic transactions made abroad when you receive your next statement back home. Try not to carry money, chequebook, cards, travellers' cheques, passport, and keys all together in the same container whether it be a bag, a purse, a wallet, or one of those ridiculous "bum bags" that encourage people to do just the wrong thing. The latest fashion amongst young women, the bag worn like a school satchel on the back, must be every thief's dream come true!

Be especially careful on beaches and take with you only what is absolutely necessary. With the present trend for designer labels not even your clothing is safe when you go in for a swim.

Whenever possible use the hotel safe to store valuable items and documents and never leave anything of value in the room. Although staff are usually very honest, it is quite simple for strangers to walk around hotels now that more and more of them have bars, restaurants and even swimming pools open to the general public. Rooms are usually left open by the cleaning staff as they strip the beds and change towels, etc.

It is not unknown for thieves to stay one night in an hotel, get a copy of the room key made, and then visit at their leisure to ransack the room knowing the occupant has gone to the beach or off on a sightseeing trip organised by the hotel.

If you are tempted to go native in Amsterdam, or anywhere else, and hire a bicycle, make sure that when you chain it to the railings you do so through the front wheel and the frame. A mate of mine came out of the pub one night and found only the front wheel still padlocked to the lamppost, the rest of the bike had disappeared.

Be especially careful when travelling because crime on the roads and railways is on the increase almost everywhere abroad. Thieves have been known to spray powerful sleeping-gases under the doors of compartments on trains in Europe and then steal from the unfortunate occupants. Short of barricading oneself into the compartment it is difficult to defend against this kind of robbery.

Diversion tactics are often used against unwary motorists. Tyres are deliberately punctured when the vehicle is parked at a filling station or café, and while one or two members of the gang assist with changing the wheel another member will be helping himself to anything valuable he can lay his hands on. He will then puncture another tyre so that you will be unable to follow them on discovering you have been robbed. This type of crime is especially prevalent in Spain and Italy at the moment.

Breaking the law abroad
It is not only the locals who commit offences overseas. Farmers in Switzerland long ago ceased putting cowbells on their herds because

the bells were frequently stolen as souvenirs by tourists.

Should you be unfortunate enough to fall foul of the law on foreign soil do not expect too much help from the British Consulate. From my experience I have found them to be sadly lacking in sympathy and devoid of any sense of humour. In Saudi Arabia I knew personally men who were involved in traffic accidents, in which they were entirely blameless, and yet locked up by the Saudi authorities. If they were fortunate enough to have been in Jeddah (where the embassy is situated) at the time of the accident, they may have been lucky enough to have received a visit from some lowly official. If the accident occurred across the Kingdom in Dhahran or Riyadh they were just left to rot as far as the British authorities were concerned. It was the employer that had to plead and provide for the prisoner, and eventually pay to get him released.

Prison in most Middle East countries is a far cry from what constitutes punishment in UK jails. Firstly, in a lot of places prisoners are not fed by the authorities. Food has to be brought in by relatives or friends. Should the poor soul be devoid of the same, he is allowed out of prison, with an escort, to beg for money to buy food. When he has enough for a loaf of bread and a bit of cheese he is locked up again.

The British media is responsible for much exaggeration when describing the punishment meted out by Saudi Arabian courts. Thieves only have the right hand chopped off after persistently offending. For the first offence it is usually a fine that is followed by a prison sentence then corporal punishment for subsequent offences. It is only after refusing to learn by past mistakes that the offender is awarded the ultimate punishment.

The beating, or *laying on of the lash,* is intended to be humiliating, not painful. The *mullah* holds a copy of the Koran under his arm whilst administering the punishment, which makes it difficult to get any power into the blows. I have read of several Brits who claim they were thrashed, (always for doing nothing illegal), but have yet to see any evidence in the way of scars or bruises to support their stories.

I do agree Saudi law can sometimes appear brutal. For highjacking an aircraft the punishment is immediate execution on landing, without the chance of a trial. Women that commit adultery are still stoned to death, although I heard that the present way of carrying out the sentence is more in keeping with the Saudis' emergence from the dark ages. They now use a lorry to tip ten tons of rocks on the unfortunate woman.

It is easy to break the law overseas without even knowing it, as a friend of mine discovered after a road accident in Germany. A back wheel came off his car when a half shaft snapped and he ended up in a ditch after ploughing through half a dozen saplings at the side of the road. He duly reported the accident to the local police station to cover himself with the insurance company back home and promptly forgot about the matter. He was most surprised a few days later to receive a visit from the local constabulary charging him with failing to report the damage to the trees. It transpires that all trees in Germany are owned by some authority, council or government, and when damaged must be replaced. It added a further few hundred marks to his claim.

The same friend fell foul of the law in Osnabruck shortly afterwards. Approaching a railway level crossing in the centre of town, he was taken by surprise when the barrier started to come down. His first reaction was to put his foot down and attempt to beat the train. Realising in time that he was not going to be successful, he hit the brakes and came to a screeching halt inches from the barrier. A local policeman, in his ankle-length green leather overcoat ambled across the road and removing his baton from his belt, proceeded to thump the roof of the car leaving six perfectly spaced ridges. He then ambled off again without saying a word. I suppose the British number plates convinced him that an on-the-spot fine would not be sufficient punishment.

The strangest on-the-spot punishments I ever saw meted out were on the Ikorodu Road in Lagos, once reckoned to be the most dangerous road on the planet. In an attempt to cut down on the number of road deaths, metal walkways were built across the four-lane highway. In the heat and humidity of the West African climate, the climb up the steps and the long trudge across was often considered too much of an effort by a lot of the indigenous population. They were quite prepared to risk their lives dodging the endless streams of lorries, cars, taxis, motorbikes, and mammy wagons roaring down the road.

However, on arriving at the other side, the pedestrian that was lucky enough to have made it, was often met by a member of the local police force. With his large, hob-nailed boots, he would kick the unfortunate offender viciously on both shins, then force him to hobble across the walkway back to where he had just come from. It was certainly a case of making the punishment fit the crime.

It is surprisingly easy to fall foul of the law abroad. Many travellers, on seeing trees festooned with fresh fruit are tempted to pick something. However, unless it is a cactus pear you are picking a hundred miles from the nearest building, you can bet your boots someone will appear and claim ownership of the fruit. And demand payment.

Longer ago than I now care to remember, I was strolling in the gardens of the Federal Palace Hotel in Lagos. It was a hot afternoon but there was a stiff breeze blowing in from the sea. Suddenly there was an earth-shattering thump behind me and I turned to discover a coconut had fallen from a palm and missed me by no more that five feet. Coconuts, in their natural state, are in a husk and about three times the size, and weight, as when seen in the shops. It is generally believed that, worldwide, falling coconuts are responsible for around a thousand deaths every year. In fact, you are ten times more likely to be killed by a coconut than by a shark!

Thanking my lucky stars, I stooped and picked the thing up with the idea of showing it to my mates at the bar and explaining how lucky I had been. I had not walked ten paces when I was confronted by a gardener and accused of stealing the coconut, which he declared in no uncertain terms was the property of the hotel. I have often since wondered would the hotel have been so quick to claim ownership if the thing had landed on my head?

Strange as it may seem, America is the most likely place to get locked up. More Brits are imprisoned there, per number of visitors, than any other holiday destination. However, more British nationals die in Spain than anywhere else, mostly from natural causes.

It is an offence to attempt to import alcohol or pornography into many Muslim countries, and this fact is well known by most travellers, but there are other countries with quite remarkable and lesser-known laws.

For example, a man may be arrested for wearing a skirt in Italy (bad news for a certain British footballer). In Spain it is an offence to whistle on a bus or train, while in France a farmer could go to prison for naming a pig Napoleon. In Germany it is against the law to wear a mask, especially in a bank holding a gun! You can also be fined on the spot for jaywalking, even if there is no traffic about. In the USA bottles of spirits must be wrapped when carried in a public place, although cans of beer can be openly drunk on the streets. In Oman it is an offence to drive a dirty car. If that law was introduced in the UK 90% of farmers and farm workers would have to be locked up.

Singapore is one of the few places on earth where it is perfectly safe to drink the water straight from the tap but the local byelaws there are somewhat Draconian. Chewing gum is forbidden and importation of the same can result in a fine of almost £1,000. A few years ago an American youth was sentenced to six strokes of the cane on his bare buttocks and a £1,400 fine for vandalising cars. After a direct appeal from President Clinton the six strokes were reduced to four. Drug trafficking is punishable by death and around a hundred smugglers have been executed in the last twenty years. However, the streets of Singapore are among the cleanest and safest on earth. Muggings are unheard of and one can roam the streets all day and night quite safely, but beware of falling TV sets!

To sum up, be careful, and be warned that you will not receive much sympathy if you do break the law overseas, especially from the British Embassy.

Airsmiles 2
Wanting to sue an airline for damage to his luggage, a man visited a solicitor. He was informed his case was not strong enough.

CHAPTER THREE

Arriving

The arrival

Your first problem on arrival at your destination is to get through
Immigration, Customs, and sometimes Health Control. At the majority
of European and American airports there is little or no problem as
things are generally well organised. There can, however, be the matter
of long queues, especially if arriving early in the morning at an
international airport. Because of noise regulations aircraft are not
permitted to land before certain times, and this can lead to a number
of flights arriving within minutes of one-another as soon as the airfield
opens. With the number of passengers a present day jumbo jet is able
to carry, it can mean many hundreds of people attempting to clear
Immigration at the same time.

Make sure you join the correct queue. At all international airports
there are separate entrances for nationals and foreign visitors and
there could also be separate entrances for foreign visitors with Resident
Permits, or holding Common Market Passports. Usually the gates are
well signposted so it worthwhile spending a few extra seconds looking
around rather than rushing blindly to join a queue only to find when
arriving at the head of it you are in the wrong one and have to start
again.

Be sure to have a visa if one is required for the country being
visited. Your travel agent will be able to advise you whether or not one
is needed. You could, if necessary, telephone the embassy of the
country concerned before travelling if you are not certain. It is possible
to obtain visas at the airport in some countries such as Egypt and
Uganda, but this practice is not to be recommended as it is time
consuming and can leave one open to abuse from an unscrupulous
official. It is also, invariably, more expensive.

For countries that do require visas make sure that you apply in
plenty of time before your departure date. Some visas can take several

weeks to obtain. For some countries, Russia for example, it is possible to apply for visas on the Internet.

Arrival in most countries without a visa will mean refusal to enter, or in Libya, a night in detention as I know from experience!

If your journey includes a stopover in another country en route, or even just a change of aircraft, make sure that you have a transit visa if required. Once again, your travel agent should be able to supply all the relevant information.

The regulations concerning transit visas for different countries would fill another chapter, as they are quite complicated. If flying through Russia, for example, en route to Armenia, Azerbaijan, Belarus, etc., you will require one if stopping off. There is a list of forty countries whose residents require transit visas for the UK even if they are in Direct Airside Transit. That means not even leaving the airfield or going through Immigration.

The USA also has strict rules on passengers from overseas flying via Miami to South America and the Caribbean. Once again, the Internet is very helpful in this respect.

Immigration forms will have to be completed for most countries outside the EEC and are usually handed out by the cabin crew well before arrival at your destination. They are quite simple to fill in and usually just request name, passport details, and the address of where you expect to stay. Sometimes they may also ask for your profession. If you are a medical man I advise you not to admit it once you have arrived at your hotel, because, should your fellow guests discover the fact, every breakfast time could turn out to be a morning surgery.

You may find when arriving at places such as Cairo, Lagos, and many others around the world that there are obliging characters who will offer to get you through the formalities of arrival without you having to join any queues. It will, of course, cost you money. First and foremost you should never hand over your passport to any unauthorised person and secondly, although they will probably get you through Immigration quickly on the way into the country, you could find yourself in big trouble when you come to leave again if all the right stamps are not in your passport.

There are, of course, perfectly legitimate representatives from various travel agents, tour operators, etc., who will look after immigration formalities for you if you are one of their clients.

Customs clearance can vary from the virtually non-existent as in travel between EEC countries, to minute scrutiny of all baggage and possible body searches as in Saudi Arabia, Israel and other sensitive areas. The only thing to do is to ensure that you are not breaking any local regulations concerning contraband, and be patient.

All alcohol is forbidden in Saudi Arabia and Libya and passengers attempting to smuggle any spirits in are subject to deportation, and possibly worse. Videotapes and medical supplies are also viewed with suspicion. You will also discover that newspapers such as the *Sun* and the *News of the World* are not allowed into many Muslim countries. The in-flight magazine is usually a good source of information regarding what can be imported at your destination.

A quick word of advice to lady passengers; if you wish to spare your blushes, and those of the Customs Officer, place the more intimate articles of your clothing and personal hygiene at the bottom of your case. I have seen no end of frillies that look as if they were scooped off the bathroom floor and thrown in just before the case was closed. I can assure would-be smugglers that smelly socks and dirty undies do not deter a good Customs Officer.

Not many countries now have an active Health Control at the airport but still be prepared to show your documents if required to. However, if you are arriving from a country that has had an epidemic of one kind or another you could find yourself being led away for an inoculation if your medical documents do not show the necessary immunisation.

On returning home from an overseas trip always be alert for any possible illness that may have been picked up abroad. It is not possible to be immunised against all the maladies that lurk in distant deserts and jungles. Some can take weeks, months, or even years to make their presence felt. I feel enough has been said about the AIDS virus in the media to make it unnecessary for me to comment further

Having come safely through all controls and been happily reunited with your luggage you now find yourself on the pavement outside the airport in a strange land. Be prepared for anything.

Transportation
At almost every airport on earth you will find taxis lining up waiting for passengers. At Tel Aviv, in Israel however, it is not so. You will have to turn right outside the arrivals hall and walk a hundred yards to find a taxi car park. It is well organised with a kiosk to report to, but still not convenient when one is lugging a heavy suitcase and it is pouring with rain.

All the best hotels everywhere have courtesy buses that wait at the airport exit and transport you directly to your hotel. Virgin Airlines lay on limousines for the convenience of Upper Class passengers. I was most surprised on returning from Miami to be driven from Gatwick to Reading Station at no extra charge. Other airlines have arrangements with certain car hire firms so if you are thinking of renting a vehicle it is worth making enquiries before you catch the flight. The car is ready for you to pick up at your destination and transport to the car park is supplied.

Be extremely careful when selecting a taxi abroad, especially if travelling alone. In places as diverse as New York and Lagos there are accounts of travellers being driven to remote sites and robbed, or worse. If possible share a cab with another passenger or ask a porter to recommend a taxi having tipped him generously and noted his badge number. Never hail a taxi in the street, unless it's a yellow cab in New York city, a black cab in London, or one equally recognisable as an official hackney carriage which are generally reckoned to be safe. Always get the hotel porter or the barman to phone for a taxi for you.

Beware also of "cowboy cabbies" that are just as likely to be found in Britain as elsewhere. They usually operate with the assistance of a tout who waits at airports and railway stations and offers to get you to the front of the taxi rank. You will invariably be charged an extortionate price for your ride.

Whenever possible, in a cab without a meter, agree a price before getting in the vehicle. If the taxi has a meter fitted make sure that it is switched on.

Women travelling alone should be especially careful when taking taxis. I was staggered to read that in 1997 sixteen women passengers were raped in London minicabs, and sixty-six others sexually assaulted! If you are not safe in London what chance do you have in places like Lagos, Bangkok, or New York? It must be said that anyone using a minicab in London instead of a proper taxi is asking for trouble.

London is the only place in the whole of the UK where minicabs are unlicensed. Any convicted robber or rapist is free to open up a minicab business in the capital. I do believe at last there are moves afoot to get this anomaly rectified — the sooner the better.

In some places the taxis are run like buses and will pick up other passengers en route unless you are prepared to pay extra for exclusive service. A brief word on buses; outside Europe, North America, and the Antipodes I do not recommend them. I have seen the most appalling accidents involving "mammy wagons" in Nigeria and various modes of transport purporting to be public service vehicles in the Middle East and other far flung locations. In Bangladesh I truly believe all bus drivers have a death wish, or else the fumes from the dilapidated vehicles have addled their brains. They hurtle between villages with horns blaring scattering livestock, pedestrians, and other road users willy-nilly. As the roads are generally in a deplorable state with only enough surface left to accommodate a single vehicle, a car driver can expect to spend the greater part of any journey with his nearside wheels off the road.

I do know of some people, including my wife, who actually enjoyed travelling on local buses in Africa, but for my own part I remain convinced that it is not the way I wish to travel.

A possible exception could be Malta where they still use old British single deck buses built in the fifties. They are kept in good mechanical order and are wonderfully decorated inside with religious icons. I once asked a driver why he sat to one side of the driving seat and was informed that the space left was "for God, who is really driving the bus". Regardless of whoever was driving, it was extremely good value for money. A few years ago it was possible to travel from Valetta to Sliema for just a few pence, and anywhere on the island for less than a pound.

In Asia one will come across many strange forms of transport including rickshaws, rickshaw bicycles, and baby taxis. The latter are Vespacars, which as the name suggests, are basically scooters with a car body attached. In Dhaka it is estimated there are 200,000 various forms of taxi plying for trade. The city is constantly shrouded in a dense choking fog of exhaust fumes which actually cut down the effect of the sun's rays and keep the town a degree or two cooler that the surrounding countryside. For my part, I'll accept the extra heat and the clear air that goes with it. The city's policemen wear anti-smog masks to prevent themselves being suffocated by the fumes that constantly envelop them.

No matter how many times I used a rickshaw bicycle I could never feel comfortable at the fact I was making another human being struggle to transport me from one place to another. I always eased my conscience by tipping the man far too generously, often to the chagrin of one of the locals who was accompanying me.

Before electing to take a taxi it is advisable to make sure there is not a train or bus service into town that will be considerably cheaper.

Having got into a taxi and onto the road the best thing to do in most places is lie back and shut your eyes. The standard of driving of a lot of overseas taxi drivers is diabolical. Anywhere in Africa, with the possible exception of some South African cities, a taxi ride is a nightmare. In Rome or Riyadh, Paris or Panama, Cairo or Kano, one can get out of a taxicab as a shivering wreck.

I recently read of a taxi driver in India whose vehicle became stuck in reverse gear. He has since gone on to clock up 7,500 miles going backwards! How desperate does one have to be for a lift to hire a cab that cannot go forwards?

The journey into Lagos from Mutallah Muhammed Airport takes one along the Ikorodu Road. At one time this road was listed in the Guinness Book of Records as having more accidents than any other road in the world. The building of overhead walkways has considerably reduced the carnage but, occasionally, a dead body can still be seen lying in the road.

I believe the title for the most dangerous stretch of road on earth is now held by the M125 in Portugal. This is the main route to the Algarve for the hundreds of thousands of tourists that visit the place every summer. At the last count it was estimated that the annual death toll for this road was one death for every 1,000 metres. The fact that the punishment for drink driving in Portugal is usually a £40 fine does not go a long way to improving the situation.

However, to return to Africa, in the late seventies the traffic congestion was so bad in Lagos that the government was forced to take drastic action to combat it. The scheme they came up with was that on Mondays, Wednesdays, and Fridays vehicles with an even number registration plate were allowed into town, and on Tuesdays, Thursdays, and Saturdays odd numbered registration plates were allowed in. Sunday was open to all. The system worked all right for a couple of weeks but, by then, most drivers were operating on two different numberplates so congestion was as bad as ever.

It seems that things have not improved much in Nigeria in the last twenty years. In 2003 a total of 608 Nigerian motorists were tested for insanity after being caught driving against the flow of traffic in Lagos, although flowing is not how I recall the movement of traffic there.

Of the 608, one person was found to be insane and twenty were found to be of very low intelligence indicating that they were not fit to drive. In my opinion one would have to be mad to want to drive in Lagos anyway!

Driving anywhere in Nigeria is to say the least, interesting. There are now highways out of Lagos to Abeocuta, Ibadon, and Benin, but the roads to distant places such as Kano, Onitsha, and Port Harcourt are still fraught with danger. In the seventies armed robbers, mostly in army uniforms, were everywhere. With the aid of public executions held on the beach at weekends, this problem has now eased but not been entirely eradicated. The roads themselves are also a problem as no one seems to have discovered a way to prevent them being eroded every rainy season. The earth of Nigeria is mainly red laterite that washes away with the rain causing the sides of the highway to collapse. This usually leaves a strip of asphalt down the centre of the road along which huge trucks thunder scattering lesser vehicles into the bush. When meeting a truck of equal size coming from the opposite direction each driver will immediately assume the other man will give way, with catastrophic results. I have seen two Mercedes trucks embedded in one another in the centre of a long, single lane bridge.

The standard of Nigerian driving was summed up for me by the representative of an American drugs company who stated; "You Brits ruined the birth control market when you taught the Nigerians to drive!"

Women travelling by road in Africa should be prepared to see naked local men standing in rivers soaping and shampooing themselves. African women seem to be more discreet in their ablutions but can still be seen on occasions. Men and women, however, will seemingly relieve themselves anywhere. It is not uncommon in many African towns to see notices such as "Do not urinate here" on walls of banks and other business premises.

The traffic jams in Bangkok are horrendous. Drivers spend so much time in their cars that some carry gadgets to meet their physical needs. One such gadget is the Comfort 100, a portable lavatory that is on sale at most garages. I read recently that a similar device is now available in the UK. If desperate, I think I'd prefer to go the Nigerian way!

If you intend driving overseas do check with the travel agent that your licence is valid in the country, or countries, that you intend visiting. Most countries will permit tourists to drive on a national licence, but for an extended stay an international licence may be required. Some places, such as Libya, require all visitors working in the country to have a local licence. Also advise your insurance company if you intend to take your vehicle out of the UK. You may be called upon to pay an extra premium. The amount to be paid will depend on where you intend visiting, and for how long.

In Spain and Italy, if driving your own vehicle, you will need an International Driving Permit. In Spain, you will also need a bail bond that is obtainable from your insurance company.

You will also have to have the headlights on your car adjusted for driving on the "wrong" side of the road. I know many tourists visit the continent without troubling to do this but it is an offence, and one that is increasingly being picked up by the local constabulary. It is a very simple matter to attach stick-on beam deflectors that are available from most car accessories shops, or from the AA or RAC.

In continental Europe you are also legally required to carry certain items of equipment. The list varies from country to country but generally includes a First Aid kit, fire extinguisher, warning triangle, an empty fuel can and sometimes a spare bulb kit.

If your language skills permit, it is well worth reading the local papers in Germany and France as many of them announce when and where the police are about to set up speed traps. It could save you a euro or two.

The French Government recently declared that Whit Monday is no longer a public holiday and that people should turn up for work. I suggest you take this with a pinch of salt. Office staff may turn up but don't expect to find too many shops and garages open.

With all the trouble involved in taking one's own car abroad I find it far simpler to hire one locally. Many big companies that in the past would ship out Landrovers for overseas contracts now find it easier and cheaper to hire 4x4s from a local dealer for the length of the project. There is no problem with maintenance, repairs, insurance, depreciation, or customs, and at the outset it is known exactly what the transport bill will be; so many vehicles at so much for so many weeks.

Young children in cities everywhere run car protection rackets. On parking your vehicle you will be confronted by a smiling youngster who will offer to guard it for you for a few cents, kobo, lira, or whatever the local currency is. Pay him and your car will be safe, pay him a little extra and he will even wash the vehicle for you. Fail to pay him and you are sure to return to a flat tyre, missing hubcaps, or worse. It is frustrating being held to ransom this way, but as a local way of life one is forced to endure it.

When driving anywhere overseas be especially wary of animals. In Arab countries camels, donkeys, sheep, and goats wander much as they please. To hit one will involve much shouting, wailing, and the eventual forking out of a considerable amount of money. Any creature hit is inevitably the best in the flock/herd, or pregnant, or both. You will be expected to pay compensation for the dead animal and all its would-have been offspring. Hitting a dog in an Arab country will probably qualify you for a round of applause from any onlookers as they are largely regarded as pests.

In Africa beware of wild animals. Even creatures the size of elephants can materialise as if by magic in the road ahead. The chances of your killing an elephant are remote, the chances of him doing you irreparable damage should you hit him are extremely likely. I have seen a vehicle flattened to the height of a biscuit tin by a couple of enraged bulls. I have been informed that the best course of action on hitting an elephant is to immediately vacate the vehicle as it is widely believed that the animal vents his wrath on the car not the driver. Fortunately, I have never had to put this theory to the test, nor do I wish to.

Parking vehicles abroad requires a little more attention than parking in the multistorey car park back home. Parking near trees can be an invitation for monkeys to swarm all over the car with subsequent damage to windscreen wipers, aerials and mirrors. Parking under trees can also mean a lot of bird mess to clean off. I thought the herring gulls in North Devon were a particular nuisance until bombarded by a maribou stork in Kampala. These hideous looking birds lurk in trees and on the tops of buildings in the city when not scavenging through dustbins and rubbish tips. The result when they relieve themselves is like a kilo of lard crashing on the roof of one's car. The use of convertibles is not recommended in Kampala.

Car hire
When hiring cars overseas it is advisable to use the established companies such as Hertz and Budget, that way there should be less likelihood of breaking down miles from anywhere. If hiring from a local firm be sure to give the car a good inspection before driving off. Check the vehicle has a spare wheel in good condition and the tools necessary to change it, including a serviceable jack. Also check the insurance cover issued, especially the small print, and do not forget to

name any co-drivers. Although, obviously, it does not matter what size the print is if one does not understand the language. In the event of an accident you could find yourself liable for a hefty excess penalty, especially if the other car driver has no insurance, which is highly likely in a lot of foreign countries.

In the USA a "free" hire car is often included in a package holiday. Although the hire of the car may be free you will almost certainly discover that the insurance of the vehicle is not included. This will cost you in the region of $15 (£10+) per day.

Always make sure you are familiar with local rules and regulations. In the USA speed limits differ from state to state, and fifty miles per hour is often the limit, which is not easy to stick to if used to motorway driving. Thankfully, the American craze for "gas guzzlers" has abated somewhat and sensible sized vehicles are now readily available.

You may also find yourself liable for any damage to the vehicle. This can include minor bumps and scratches caused by other inconsiderate motorists so be especially careful where you park. In public car parks I always park next to the newest car available, and in supermarket car parks I never park close to the entrance/exit to the building. Here you are in constant danger of being struck by uncontrollable shopping trolleys being propelled by women scrutinising a metre and a half of till roll.

Make sure you are aware of the procedure for returning the car, especially out of office hours. Have the car inspected by a representative of the hire company and have any damage reported put in writing, and if paying by credit card, be sure to check your next statement to see how much was deducted. I have heard of all kinds of extras being added on to the bills of unsuspecting hirers.

For minor traffic offences the police in many African countries are reluctant to get involved in paperwork and subsequent criminal proceedings and will normally administer a punishment on the spot. For a local driver this usually means a whack with a stick or a kick in the shins; for a tourist it is more likely to be a "fine" — but do not expect a receipt.

If travelling out of town, especially in hot weather, it is advisable to carry a good supply of water, a spade, and a sturdy rope. Besides its obvious uses, in the Middle East I have found bottled water as good as currency in some situations.

While driving in towns or built up areas, should you find it necessary to know which direction north is, there is no longer any need to resort to the old hour hand at the sun routine that you learnt in your scouting days; in the northern hemisphere all satellite dishes point south, and the opposite applies in the southern hemisphere. Mind you, on the equator they point straight upwards so you will need a compass there.

If contemplating taking a hire car across the border, e.g. into Portugal from Spain, be sure to advise the car rental company in advance. Many countries use special registration numbers, or different colour plates for hire cars so that they are immediately evident as such to Immigration and Customs officials. Although your trip may be perfectly innocent, if you have not informed the rental company you could find yourself facing an attempted car theft charge. I know, I recently had a problem attempting to travel from Morocco to Gibraltar for the weekend.

In places of high risk, such as Florida seems to be at the moment, it is not advisable to advertise the fact that one is a tourist by leaving maps, brochures, and cameras on open view. Keep them in the glove compartment or the boot when not actually in use.

If driving overseas for the first time be warned that foreign drivers, on the whole, are far less courteous than British drivers. In the present climate of ever increasing reports of incidents of road rage this may be hard to believe but it is generally true. In most African and Arab countries it is considered a weakness to give way to another driver attempting to join traffic from the side. At traffic lights one should be prepared to be assailed by a cacophony of car horns one nanosecond after the lights turn to green if you are unfortunate enough to be first on the grid. A change of lights is like the start of a Formula 1 grand prix.

Be very careful of flashing headlight signals. In the UK it is usually a sign that the other driver is giving way for you to cross in front or for you to join the traffic ahead. Overseas it invariably means *get out of my way*. I have always found that the best policy is to drive like the natives, being courteous only upsets them as they are not prepared for it.

Do not always expect traffic lights to be stood on the corner at street level. Many countries, especially the USA, delight in suspending lights from overhead cables. These can be hard to spot if the sun visor is down or when driving through a well-lit street at night.

In Zimbabwe they refer to this kind of traffic light as a robot. I know, having had a very interesting chat with a local policeman at half past one in the morning having failed to notice a red one in the pouring rain.

Road signs are usually international and therefore simple to understand, but the speed limits will be written in local numerals. The AA or RAC will be able to supply the relevant translations for whatever country is to be visited.

Should the worse happen and you do get involved in an accident I am afraid you will have to deal with it as you see fit. I have certainly driven in places where the best thing to do if you hit a person, or an animal, is to keep driving until the next town is reached and report the accident there. I know of instances where a driver has been beaten and burnt alive inside his vehicle after killing a child that ran into the road in Nigeria.

It will also be helpful if you know what fuel to look for when you are driving overseas. In France, for example, you will find the following:

Sans plomb	Unleaded petrol
Ordinaire	Leaded 2 star
93 octane	Leaded 3 star
Super	Leaded 4 star
Diesel	Gazoil

Any decent phrase book for whatever country you are visiting should contain similar information.

Trains
When travelling long distances overseas there is a lot to be said for letting the train take the strain. In many African countries such as Kenya, Uganda, Zimbabwe, and South Africa there are very good

railway systems which provide both an excellent mode of transport and also a wonderful way to see the country, and virtually the whole of the Indian subcontinent can be explored using the steam engines which have been operating since the days of the *Raj*.

Most European countries can boast of railway networks to better those now to be found in the UK. A trip on the American Amtrac is a luxury compared to a journey on Intercity.

The French TGV (high speed train) that can reach speeds of 186 mph, is a delight to travel on, as indeed are all the French trains. You are allocated a carriage and seat number at time of booking so know exactly where to wait on the platform for easy access to the train. The ticket collectors on board are always polite and greet every passenger with a *bonjour*.

You may also be pleasantly surprised at the cheapness of foreign rail travel. In Morocco, where they use French-built, electric locomotives, the cost of a first class ticket from Rabat to Casablanca, approximately 100km, is less than £5 return.

The midnight train which runs four hundred miles across Northern Russia from St Petersburg to Moscow is the height of luxury and costs less than £40 first class. Included in the price are a two-bed compartment and a pre-packed breakfast with coffee. It also manages to arrive bang on time at 7.15 a.m. throughout the year. In winter it ploughs through snowdrifts at temperatures of minus 10C. The British rail operators could learn a lot from their Russian counterparts.

A more expensive, but equally exciting journey is the two-day trip from Vancouver to Banff in Canada on the Rocky Mountaineer. The scenery through the Rockies is awesome.

Some years ago, on a long journey in Germany, such as the one from Munich to Hamburg, some trains were equipped with seats the backs of which pulled down to form a bed. It was quite surprising to find oneself suddenly lying down to sleep next to a complete stranger. It is over ten years since I last travelled on the DBB so am not sure if this sleeping arrangement is still available. It will be a shame if it is not as it was a certain way to get to know your fellow travellers.

Be careful when buying a ticket for travel on a German train, you may have to pay extra for the faster trains. I paid what I considered was the normal fare for a trip from Osnabruck to Aachen and was then informed by the ticket collector I was on a *snellzug,* the express, so had to cough up extra *marks* for the privilege. If in no hurry take the slow train and enjoy the views, especially if travelling in Bavaria where the scenery is breathtaking.

In Italy they also have different charges for different kinds of trains.

I recall once going from Rome to Bari on a train fitted out with wooden seats; a journey I have no wish to repeat.

At large stations such as Aachen which is close to the border, it is quite common for trains of France or some other country, to be united with a train of Germany before continuing its onward journey. This can involve a lot of shuffling backwards and forwards of various carriages and can be quite alarming if you are not certain of what is going on. I was myself once panic-stricken, having alighted to get some refreshment, to turn and see my train steaming out of the station ten minutes ahead of time. Fortunately, it returned three minutes later to connect to the extra carriages brought to the platform.

If travelling across borders in a train be prepared for Customs inspections. I have always found the officers on trains to be far more intimidating than their counterparts at airports. I remember crossing the Belgian/German border as a young serviceman and having to turn out the contents of my case onto the seat. The two Belgian officers then proceeded to help themselves to two jars of coffee that I was taking back as presents for German friends. They told me it was illegal to take coffee across the border and I was in no position to argue with them. To this day I still believe the so-and-sos stole my coffee.

A very good money saving scheme in the Dutch capital is the Amsterdam Saver, available from Tourist Information Offices. For 26 euros, around £18, you get twenty-four hours unlimited travel on underground, bus, and tram networks and free admission to all the major museums.

Airsmiles 3

At an air show a man paid to go for a spin in a small, two-seater aeroplane. The pilot did a corkscrew climb, a victory roll, looped the loop, and concluded with a falling leaf. As they hurtled to the ground he turned to his passenger, "Half the people down there think we are going to have an accident" chuckled the pilot.

"Half the people up here *have* had an accident" came the mournful reply.

CHAPTER FOUR

Accommodation

Hotels

Accommodation abroad comes literally in all shapes and sizes, and all conditions, so be most careful when booking in advance. Everyone is aware of examples of tourists arriving at the hotel to find the builders still completing it.

Whilst staying in foreign accommodation do not always assume that the hot water tap will be the left hand one and the cold tap the right one. I have on several occasions found myself cleaning my teeth in almost boiling water after running what I assumed would be the cold tap. Also, you cannot always believe what it says on the tap. Always assuming that you know the local language for hot and cold.

In the late sixties and early seventies, when the oil rich Middle East countries began spending their newly acquired wealth, they bought articles from all over the world. Whatever took their fancy would be shipped back home. Hence it was not unusual to find yourself in a luxurious villa with an Italian bathroom and French kitchen appliances. The local tradesmen had no idea what the French and Italian was for hot and cold so took pot luck when installing them. The French word for warm is chaud which means even if the local plumber got it right the hot tap would have a "c" on it, which is confusing enough.

Water tanks were always installed on the roof where in summer the temperature would reach over 100 degrees Fahrenheit. It took quite a time to get used to the idea that there was never going to be any cold water from either tap.

Also purchased abroad in vast amounts by traveling Arabs were luxury items. As electronics engineers we were always being requested to repair electrical equipment that the Saudi Air Force personnel had brought back from the USA and plugged into the local supply. The US runs on 120 volts domestic supply. Most of the rest of the world, including Saudi Arabia, runs on 240 volts. We had a hell of a job explaining that some items like clocks and computers, purchased in the USA would never run properly in Saudi Arabia because, just to be different, American mains are 60 cycles, not 50 cycles like everyone else.

I was fortunate enough to have stayed in some beautiful villas during my time overseas, especially in Libya. The country was once a colony of Italy so there is a lot of Italian influence in the architecture. Marble is used in copious amounts, which is all very well in the summer, but can strike cold in the winter months. Even with all the marble, I remember some nights in Libya when it was just too hot to sleep indoors.

At weekends during the day we would drag our mattresses onto the flat roof that is always a feature of the new villas, and sunbathe. Meals would be served by Jusef the houseboy washed down by contraband beer manufactured by the expat nurses in the local hospitals. By the time the sun went down in the evening we would all be in reflective mood. I recall some very strange conversations going on as I lay back and contemplated the stars glittering in the velvety blackness of the clear night sky.

"Why does the moon look so much bigger here than back in the UK?" was one rather sensible question.

"Because it is ten feet deep in dead flies" was the not so sensible reply of some Brit as he viciously swiped at another insect that had dared invade his personal space.

This prompted another would-be philosopher to ask, "What's the last thing that goes through a fly's mind when he hits your windscreen?"

Before I could suggest "thoughts of the hereafter" or something equally profound, the questioner supplied the answer, "His rear end!"

This provoked more discussion. Would this be equally true for any direction? We were, after all, all qualified engineers. We finally agreed it would be true for a head-on hit, or one from directly behind. Hit amidships (word obviously supplied by one of our ex naval men), it could not be true. So were many very happy hours passed under the Mediterranean sun, and moon.

It was always very pleasant when walking around Tripoli on a hot, dusty day to turn a corner and suddenly find oneself in a cool, leafy courtyard, so obviously a leftover of the "bad" old colonial days. Other reminders were to be found out of town. When driving south from Tripoli in the fertile crescent north of the Sahara Desert, one would see ruined homes and abandoned vineyards, reminders of the Italian colonists who toiled there before World War II. Because of the ban on alcohol there is no interest in the vineyards. Enough grapes are grown in smallholdings for the local markets.

I have stayed in hotels, motels, boarding houses, private houses, caravans, portacabins, and aboard ship. I have slept more hours than I care to think about in aircraft all over the globe. I have also tried, unsuccessfully, to sleep on trains. Not in a compartment, but in a proper sleeper. I'm not sure if is is any different now, but the last time I booked a sleeper with British Rail I found I shared the compartment with a complete stranger. I prefer the American system where you all bunk down together. There is something to be said about safety in numbers. Fortunately, I have not had to spend time under canvas but have slept in a vehicle on the odd occasion.

I only spent one month aboard a ship, cruising up and down the Mediterranean Sea, and it was absolute hell. I was not on a cruise ship but a seismic survey vessel; the *Lucien Cayron*. We were searching for likely oil-drilling areas in the Bay of Sirte off the north Libyan coast. The search involved firing off an explosion every fifteen seconds and then recording the echoes as they bounced back from the ocean floor. This process went on for twenty-four hours a day, weather and equipment permitting. I used to pray for bad weather just to get a break from the constant thump of the explosions. It was surprising how often my prayers were answered. The Med can get really wild at times.

The excitement of the survey was further enhanced by the presence of the American Sixth Fleet. We would be constantly shadowed by a warship, usually a frigate, and regularly buzzed by fighters from one of the carriers. The ship and most of the crew were French but the fact we were in Libyan waters was excuse enough for the Yanks to harass us.

I was aboard the *Lucien Cayron* when the Chernobyl Nuclear Power Station disaster took place. When we heard the news (now known to have been greatly exaggerated) of a cloud of contamination spreading across Europe we were very grateful to be where we were off the coast of Africa.

I must admit I prefer hotels to other forms of accommodation. After toiling somewhere in the tropics all day the last thing I wish to do is cook for myself and wash a pile of sweaty clothes. I am not keen on motels as I have never felt secure in them, which can probably be attributed to Alfred Hitchcock and "Psycho". On the other hand I have definite reasons for not liking portacabins and caravans as I have always found them either too hot or too cold, and no matter what one uses in the way of insecticides little creatures seem to thrive in these types of dwellings.

I once spent ten weeks living in a large caravan at Kasane, Botswana.

The site was beside the Chobe River, well known for its wildlife including hippos and crocodiles that often draped themselves along the river bank. All night long I would hear animals slinking, scampering, and slithering across the roof as I attempted to get to sleep. I swear there was a greater variety of creatures performing nightly on the roof of my cabin than ever appeared in a Chipperfield's three ring circus. In the morning I dreaded walking out of the front door for fear of something horrible dropping onto my head.

My fears were not allayed by Tommy of McAlpines informing me that he had found a green mamba sunning itself on his doorstep as he attempted to leave for the site one morning. He had retreated rather sharply, slamming the door behind him. He refused to emerge until someone actually stood on the step and banged his door to prove the creature had disappeared.

Hotels, on the other hand, do provide some defence against Nature's not so welcome wonders but they cannot be judged solely on the number of stars awarded. I have stayed in five star establishments where the service was deplorable, and starless hotels where I was treated like a lord. In fact, I take little notice of the number of stars a hotel has been awarded. In 1969, en route to Saudi Arabia, I was one of five personnel who stayed the night at the Bristol Hotel in Beirut. The following morning, after dining on paella the night before, four of us went down with food poisoning. I am certain that was a five star hotel. I say was, because I heard the hotel was demolished in the troubles there, although it has probably been reconstructed by now.

I have stayed in hotels where they have insisted on changing the sheets every day even though I have said it is not necessary. On the other hand, I have heard of establishments where the sheets have been only ironed after a guest has left and then replaced in the bed ready for the next client. Years ago, commercial travellers as they were then known, would always pour a drop of tea or coffee on the sheet under the pillow to warn the next customer the sheet was second-hand!

To be fair, I have to admit living in a seaside resort as I do, that I hear some horrendous tales of guests from some hoteliers and guesthouse proprietors. I have heard of bed linen having to be thrown away after visitors have gone to sleep without bathing after returning from the beach covered in sand, suntan lotion, and even crude oil that they have trodden in on the beach. And you would not believe half the articles that people have left behind in the beds.

The day before I am due at any hotel I always advise them, by fax if possible, that I will be arriving, even though everything was confirmed weeks before. No matter how well organised an hotel is there is always something unforseen that can arise. By giving them twenty-four hours' notice I give them a chance to make other arrangements should it be necessary.

I remember on one occasion arriving with my wife at the Port Van Kleive, a small family hotel in Amsterdam, having booked, and been confirmed, for one week's stay. The receptionist apologised profusely and said there had been a mix-up over bookings. Although we were perfectly welcome to stay the first three days we would have to vacate the room after this time. However, as it was the hotel's fault, they had booked us into the Krasnapolsky Hotel for the remainder of the week and would be paying the difference. Although I preferred the informality of the Port Van Kleive, I, for one, was very happy to spend four days in a five star hotel at three star prices, and I know my wife was too.

I spent one of the strangest nights of my life in the Port Van Kleive Hotel. My wife and I had been out for a meal and a quiet drink one winter night in the late seventies. However, as often happens at the quietest times, there had been a "bell ringing" session in the bar (see Chapter 6). We had returned to the hotel rather the worse for wear. I quickly undressed, cleaned my teeth and leapt into bed. My wife was in the bathroom doing what most wives do before they climb between the sheets, remove make-up, apply cream, etc.

My wife suddenly appeared at the bedside looking as though she had seen a ghost. "Come and look," she implored me. I was very loathe to climb out from under the warm bedclothes but the look of horror on her face provided the necessary impetus. I followed her into the bathroom, wondering what on earth had disturbed her so much. She said nothing, just pointed at the lavatory pan. "Look in it" she said urgently.

I carefully lifted the lid, dreading what may be awaiting me. I recoiled in horror. The bowl was full almost to the brim with foul smelling faeces and brown liquid. I dropped the lid as though it was red hot.

"Blimey, what have you done?" I demanded.

"I haven't done anything" she replied hotly, "It was just there."

I was certain it had not been there when I had used the toilet. I was not that drunk I would not have noticed something like that.

"Did you drop a toilet roll down the loo?" I asked her.

"No I did not!" she emphatically exclaimed. "It just appeared."

Deciding it was a fault with the plumbing I told her to forget about it.

"You can't just leave it" she wailed.

"Well I can't bloody take it with me" I retorted, by now having completely lost interest in the subject. "You can sit on the seat all night and stop it coming out if you wish, I'm going to bed!" I turned and left the bathroom.

"No I'm not!" she exclaimed.

Rosemarie slammed the bathroom door shut and quickly leapt into bed.

"Now turn the light off and let's get to sleep" I said.

"I'm not turning the light off," she retorted. "Suppose it overflows and comes under the door!"

I quickly fell asleep but my wife tells me she stayed awake all night staring at the bathroom door, dreading the emergence of the evil looking substance.

The next morning it had all but disappeared. A few flushes returned the pan to its original condition but it took a lot of deodorant and a generous sprinkling of aftershave around the bathroom to get rid of the stench. We heard later from reception that there had been some kind of blowback in the plumbing. Probably due to the fact Holland is such a flat country; the sewage has no gravity to help it to the sea!

It is worth knowing that if an hotel or guesthouse has confirmed your booking, then is unable to fulfill their obligation, they are obliged to arrange other accommodation at the same price. I know of a guesthouse proprietor whose wife walked out on him just days before the summer season commenced. He was unable to run the place himself as he had a garage to run, so he virtually gave the place away rather than have the hassle of finding alternative accommodation for all of his guests.

On the subject of vacating rooms, always make sure at what time you are expected to leave on your final day. This can vary enormously from nine o'clock in the morning until as late as four o'clock in the afternoon. Hotels are at liberty to charge you for an extra day if you are not ready to leave on time, but very rarely do.

I have stayed in more hotels than I care to remember, but if asked to list my three favourites I would probably say the Tour Hassan in Rabat, the Heliopoplis in Cairo, and the Nova Park in Zurich. I must admit, however, that every hotel I ever stayed at in Amsterdam was delightful, especially the Port Van Kleive and the Marriott. The Sun hotels in southern Africa are also well worth a mention.

I did spend a delightful three weeks in the Chateau Caribbean in Belize City. The speciality of the house was piping hot soup served in coconut shells. I was most pleasantly surprised to receive a Christmas card from the proprietor the year I stayed there inviting me back at any time. The problem is, the last time I went there all my expenses were paid by British Airports Authority, the next time I will have to pay myself.

Belize is like Nigeria, but only in one instance; is has a new purpose-built capital city, Belmopan, that no-one wants to move to. The Nigerians have Abuja. They stand like ghost towns in the middle of the bush. I believe, at last, the Nigerians are beginning to utilise Abuja, probably because life is now so dangerous in Lagos.

The capital at Belmopan was constructed after Belize City was badly damaged by a hurricane in 1961. It was built many miles inland so as not to be as much at risk from hurrcanes and declared the new capital in 1970. However, as there has not been a repetition of the 1961 hurricane the local inhabitants have lost the urge to move so far from their present homes. It stands almost deserted, being slowly reclaimed by the jungle.

I am not a lover of the new, all glass architecture that seems to be the vogue for most modern hotels. I prefer a door to look like a door, not a window. I still cringe when I recall the evening in Johannesburg, when returning from dining out with my wife to the Johannesburger Hotel, I crashed into the glass front of the foyer. Wearing tinted glasses just after dusk I had not realised there was a glass door there.

Not surprisingly, the worst hotels I ever stayed in were in Africa; in Nigeria especially under normal conditions I would have spent the night in the car rather than have frequented some of the rusty, tin-roofed hovels I stayed at in Ibadan. However, in the latter years of the seventies, curfews were a common occurrence in the country and one had to be off the streets from nine o'clock in the evening until dawn the following day. The police or army did not hesitate to shoot at any vehicle seen moving during this time, so it was necessary to stop at the first available place as soon as the time for curfew approached. I still have to repress a shudder as I recall the nights I spent under constant attack from cockroaches and mosquitoes. I would spend ages in the shower as soon as I got home in an effort to rid myself of the horrors of the night before.

Although I listed the Nova Park in Zurich as one of my favourite hotels, my stays there have not always gone completely without mishap. It was there that I got caught for the largest round of drinks of my life as I have recalled elsewhere in the book.

A recent survey showed that the three most expensive cities for hotel accommodation were London, Paris, and then Milan. The two cheapest were Mexico City and Sao Paolo. Obviously, only stay in European hotels if you are on an expense account!

One thing to be aware of at any hotel is the parking arrangements for cars and buses. Most hotels have their own private car parks, but there are others where you may have to use the nearest public parking facilities or even park in the road outside.

The modern trend seems to be to build hotels with underground car parking. However, it occurs to me hotel architects either drive sports cars or do not drive at all. The headroom in most underground car parks leaves a lot to be desired. When they have twenty or more floors soaring into the skies why, oh why, are they so miserly with the space below?

At the Hotel Safir in Rabat I drove down the slope into the car park and suddenly found myself wedged tight under a concrete girder. (Can girders be concrete?) Anyway, whatever the object is called it had me caught fast. I could have understood if I was driving a bus, but it was a Landrover Discovery — not the largest of vehicles by any stretch of the imagination.

Be very careful where you park in hotel car parks, especially if wishing to make an early start in the morning. The late arrivals, on finding the place either full, in total darkness, or both, will invariably park in the spot guaranteed to cause maximum mayhem. This is certainly true in underground car parks.

Many hotels will have a special, usually rear, entrance and exit for tourist coaches. However, the common procedure seems to be to arrive at the front entrance, whereupon seventy or eighty highly excited, mostly geriatric, foreigners are disgorged and left to totter around the foyer in an effort to discover what room they will be spending the night in. The following morning, usually around daybreak, the coach will be parked at the rear entrance, belching black smoke, while bleary-eyed would-be passengers stagger around the hotel with mountains of luggage trying to find out where the transport is scheduled to leave from. If traveling as a coach passenger always ensure you know exactly when the bus will be leaving and where from.

Finally, in every hotel there are bound to be rooms that are close to the kitchens, the air conditioning system, the bar, or even next to the toilets. If you do find yourself in such a place and find it intolerable, a polite request for another room may obtain a better result than yelling at the receptionist and banging the counter. Hotels are well aware that such rooms exist but they do not go out of their way to advertise the fact. When booking hotels beware of the following descriptions;

Conveniently situated — means, in the middle of town miles from the beach.

Full of character — means, the place is falling down.

Rustic retreat — means, miles from anywhere.

Rural charm — means, shared bathroom and no hot water.
Deceptively spacious — means, was once a factory or abattoir.
Compact accommodation — means, no room to swing a cat.
Lively atmosphere — means, full of lager louts.
24 hrs entertainment — means, 18-30's Club Hell hole!

Hotel staff

One thing I have learned during my travels is to try to keep on friendly terms with the hotel staff. If they are upset, they have a thousand ways of making life uncomfortable for awkward guests. I know of a Yorkshire coach driver who was particularly obnoxious to the waiters and waitresses at a seaside hotel in the West Country. They bided their time until the Friday evening before he was due to take his charges back north then they liberally sprinkled ground Exlax into his chocolate sauce at dinner. I heard he made many an unscheduled stop on his way to Harrogate the following day.

Fortunately, I have not had occasion to meet too many hotel managers; they seem to appear only when some disaster has struck. However, I do recall a very strange event concerning a hotel manager at Cowes on the Isle of Wight in 1969. I was attending a radar course with Plessey, as they were then known, and booked into a small hotel in the centre of town. I returned one afternoon to discover the owner of the hotel and the manager having a furious row that culminated in the manager being given one month's notice.

The catering industry is one where it is far better practice to dismiss immediately and pay wages in lieu rather than have a disgruntled member of staff at liberty to wreak his revenge. Thankfully, the manager did not resort to poisoning the guests as a temperamental chef may have done. In fact, it was quite the opposite. Every night after the customers had vacated the bars, the manager would throw open the cellar doors and then invite the four resident guests to help themselves to the proprietor's wines and spirits. An offer I found too good to refuse.

My only plea of mitigation is that I was recently released from ten years in Her Majesty's Forces and considered this some kind of compensation for the deprivation I had endured in uniform. Anyway, I, and the others, took full advantage of this offer and could be seen every morning, just before dawn, staggering down to the water's edge to dispose of the evidence of our crimes. Looking back, I feel the hangovers I suffered were punishment enough.

Chambermaids, like nurses, are a breed apart. All over the world I have found them to be cheerful and fun loving. Whether they are big, fat roly-poly mammas in Africa, or blonde, budding starlets in California, they all seem to be happy in their work. I have also found them to be surprisingly honest. Coins that have fallen from one's pockets and been considered too inconsequential to search for are retrieved by the chambermaid and left on the bedside locker. When in Maseru, Lesotho, I was foolish enough to leave in my hotel room a wallet containing the equivalent to one year's pay for a chambermaid; it was handed to the manager intact.

Chambermaids can, however, be tempted by perfume. A bottle left on the dressing table is likely to be sampled, but not stolen. Sharing a lift with a couple of girls who have just finished a morning shift can be overpowering if there are a number of female guests.

Receptionists can be especially helpful. Besides taking messages they are also a good source of information. Where are the best restaurants? What car hire company gives best rates? Where can one sell dollars/sterling on the black market? These are just a few of the snippets of information that can be gleaned from a helpful receptionist.

Despite doing my utmost to remain on good terms with hotel staff, I can recall one time accidentally upsetting a receptionist at the Beach

Hotel in Tripoli. I had returned to the hotel one evening to find him behind the counter with an enormous bandage over one eye. On enquiring, I was informed that on his way home the previous evening he had passed the mental asylum that is just up the road from the hotel. Having noticed a newly made, small hole in the perimeter wall he had decided to take a peep inside. Unbeknown to him, on the other side was an inmate armed with a stick that was promptly poked into the prying eye!

My bursting into laughter on being told the tale upset the receptionist no end. He also did not take too kindly to my remark that it's no wonder people say there are more out than in.

Hotels overseas are prone to moving clients without notice. At the Beach Hotel mentioned above, I had gone off to work at Colonel Gadaffi's headquarters as usual one morning, and returned to the hotel at around five o'clock in the evening to be told I had been moved out of my room and across the road to the annex. I was also informed I would not be charged any extra for the improved facilities. On checking the annex I discovered all my belongings had been transferred and placed in the drawers and wardrobes in almost the exact positions they had occupied in my hotel room. Obviously, the hotel staff were well trained in this manoeuvre.

As I now had a kitchen, sitting room, and outside balcony overlooking the sea I had no complaints. However, I was curious to discover the reason for my move and so enquired at reception where I was informed that the whole floor of the hotel had been taken over by a visiting Head of State, but the receptionist would not tell me who it was. This in itself was rather strange, as all previous visits by Heads of State had been widely advertised in advance and welcome flags had often festooned the road from the airport into town.

Later in the evening I wandered over to the main building of the hotel to make my regular phone call to the office in the USA. I had an arrangement with the hotel telephone operator whereby, for a small remuneration, he would get me an international call from one of the hotel kiosks.

The official way to make overseas calls was to visit the main telephone exchange in town, fill in a card with the details of who was calling, who was to be called, etc., hand this over with either a passport or driving licence, and then sit and wait for anything up to four hours to be connected. One was then informed in which of eight booths the call was to be taken. The next task was to shout louder than the Russian, Syrian, Italian, or Pakistani, occupying the next booth in order to be heard umpteen thousand miles away. As far as I was concerned the extra cost of the phone calls direct from the hotel was worth every dinar.

On approaching the hotel this particular evening I was surprised to find two Libyan soldiers guarding the front door. It was only by showing my official military pass, which entitled me to enter the Baba Al Azzizia barracks where I was installing radio equipment, that I gained entry. As I climbed the steps to the first floor I turned the corner and found myself face to face with Idi Amin. To be truthful, it was more face to chest — Idi Amin was a big, big man.

He was in uniform and accompanied by several of his children. Looking at his large, round jovial face it was hard to believe that this man was responsible for the death of thousands of his fellow countrymen back in Uganda.

I carried out a survey at Entebbe Airport twelve years after this meeting and the damage this man had caused to the country was still evident. The Lake Victoria Hotel would only accept payment in sterling or dollars, and one needed a briefcase full of local Ugandan shillings to fill the car tank with petrol. Local beer was one thousand shillings a bottle in the hotel. Also, the country was rife with the AIDS virus.

Amin had succeeded in turning the "Pearl of Africa" into a wasteland. Hopefully, with help from the United Nations, the hardworking Ugandans will again one day have a country that will be the envy of the rest of the continent.

It is not only in Libya that it is advantageous to get to know the hotel telephonist. In Nigeria it can also be quite traumatic to attempt to telephone overseas. Some days one can pick up the phone and be talking to London within seconds, on other occasions it can take hours. I heard the reason for this was that the Nigerian Government is notoriously late in paying the satellite leasing bills so they are often disconnected, leaving one to the mercy of old-fashioned landlines and undersea cables. This would certainly explain the erratic standard of service encountered in the country.

Besides the waiters, chambermaids, receptionists, and telephonists, it is also useful to make oneself known to the night porter. In the UK he is a useful man for putting on bets if one is not anxious to be seen frequenting the local betting shop, and can be relied on for a nightcap when the bar is shut.

Overseas the night porter can be even more useful as I discovered when in a hotel in Benin, Nigeria during the famous "Udoji" national strike of the seventies. Almost the whole country went on strike after the government failed to give pay increases to the workers as recommended by Mr Udoji, an economist. Banks, garages, shops, water and electricity authorities, and airfields all closed down. The whole country came to a standstill. Thankfully, hotel staff turned up to work, but with no electricity and little water things were primitive. Each guest was rationed to one bucketful of water per day with which to bathe, clean one's teeth, flush the toilet, and wash one's clothes as the hotel laundry had ceased to operate.

The night porter saw to it that I had the occasional extra bucket of water, supplied me with candles, and took my soiled clothes home for his wife to wash. He also mounted guard over my vehicle in the unlit car park.

Last, but not least, the hotel barman can be a very useful connection. It is surprising just what he can pick up while seemingly being completely disinterested in what is going on around him. For the price of a couple of drinks I have picked up some very useful information from various barmen. In the USA a barman can be relied upon to call a reputable taxi company as it is certainly not advisable to flag down a cruising cab after dark in many American cities.

Of course, it would be untrue to say that every hotel member of staff is scrupulously honest, and so you should always be aware of this fact and take the necessary precautions. My many dealings with hotels have made me aware of some of the little tricks played upon the more gullible of society.

The laundry staff on returning your washed items and finding the room empty, thereby missing out on the chance of a tip, will remove a small item of your clothing (a pair of socks or underpants is favourite), and then wait for you to report your loss. The missing item is promptly "discovered" and returned to its grateful owner who duly responds with a tip.

Not me. I telephone room service, report the loss, and then remove all my clothes. On hearing the knock on the door I turn on the bath taps, splash a little water on my face and chest, then wrapping a towel around myself I open the door a couple of inches. It is patently obvious to whoever is there that I am not in the position to hand over any money so, apologising ruefully, I gratefully accept my goods and close the door. After repeating this charade a couple of times the would-be conman realises he has been rumbled and your laundry will be returned intact thereafter.

Another tip regarding laundry, never hand in expensive designer gear for washing/cleaning less than two days before booking out. Always make sure you leave yourself plenty of time to trace any missing items.

Paying the bill
It pays to spend a few minutes scrutinizing the bill before settling the account in any hotel. In the UK I have had lunches attributed to my bill when I was fifty miles out of town at the time. Fortunately, I could easily prove it so was not called upon to pay. Phone and fax charges have also mysteriously appeared on my bill at a time when, as a contractor to Motorola, I had a mobile phone and unlimited free calls so no need to use a hotel telephone.

There are more subtle ways to cheat guests. A favourite trick is to put the cost of the daily paper on the bill then charge VAT on the total. Two weeks' supply of newspapers can mean an extra 80 pence to the hotel. With a two hundred-room hotel this works out to be a nice little earner for someone. Either buy your paper elsewhere or inform the receptionist in advance that you do not intend to pay VAT on it.

On the subject of phone calls remember all hotels charge above the normal rates. The difference for a ten-minute, long distance call may mean it is worth your while to walk to the lobby to use the public phone. If you are then tempted to visit the bar the money you saved on your call should pay for the first drink.

I have found it is not a good idea to charge drinks to the room when in a hotel bar because it is normally difficult to recall exactly what one consumed and how much was bought for others. It is also a fact that the barman always seems to make a mistake with the amount of drinks purchased (no way did I drink that much!). Also, if on an expense account, it can be embarrassing discussing the figures with the company's bean counter; I always left the room wondering did he have me down as an alcoholic or a crook. Probably both!

Be sure when vacating your room on the day of departure that you lock it behind you and take the key to reception. If you have left luggage in the room to be brought down by the porter the desk will arrange this for you. Even if not leaving luggage in the room make sure you have locked it before handing over the key. In certain parts of the world (too many to list), there are certain characters hovering around corridors waiting for unsuspecting guests to leave the rooms open. At best, you will suddenly be informed by the hotel cashier that a room check has revealed that you consumed the entire contents of the mini bar the previous night, at worst, that the TV and video are missing from your room, plus various items of bedding, the pictures from the wall, the light fittings, and the carpets! I have even heard of rooms being trashed after the occupants have left which involved them being arrested at the airport minutes before take-off.

Many modern hotels now have electronic room keys. They are plastic devices, much like credit cards, that can be used to open the room door and the mini bar. I ceased to have any faith in them when I saw a Nigerian open the bar in his room in a well-known London hotel with a train ticket. He claimed he would be able to drink for nothing, as his hotel card would register no entry to the mini bar. As Nigerians are notorious for knowing of any and every fiddle going I had no reason to disbelieve him.

The hotels do have a good reason to worry about theft. In the USA it has been estimated that the hotel industry loses $100 million every year to thievery by guests. Items stolen include toilet paper, tissues, towels, bed linen, bathrobes, and even TVs and clock radios. Light bulbs are also a prime target.

Unlikely items include the spyhole from the front door, toilet seats, and hinges. There is even a recorded incident in the UK of the guests disappearing with the hotel owner's dog! Guests have been caught attempting to steal a room's furnishings – a bed, dressing table, and wardrobe had been loaded on a truck.

Items left behind by guests usually prove to be far less useful. False teeth, artificial limbs, and toupees are special favourites, but it is not unheard of for one of the family to be left behind.

I think now would be a good time to offer a quick word on the subject of hotel mini bars. Inspect carefully each bottle on arrival. It is not unknown for some guests to drink the contents and then refill with water or some other liquid that closely resembles the spirit drunk. Make sure none of the seals on the bottles are broken and report immediately any that are.

Your holiday rights

In the UK the 1956 Hotel Proprietors Act lays out quite simply the obligations of the hotel and the rights of the guests. I think most people are aware that if you fail to turn up for your visit you can be held responsible for the bill, although given sufficient warning most hotels will do their best to re-let the accommodation, but may still withhold your deposit. Any decent solicitor will be familiar with the 1956 Act.

However, abroad, especially on package tours, things are far more complicated. Problems that are frequently met with abroad include the following:

Airport delays

Passengers are at the mercy of air traffic controllers, baggage handlers, aircraft serviceability, and umpteen other factors that can cause hundreds to be stranded without notice. Even if this delay lasts a week tour operators are not obliged to pay a penny in compensation. They are not even obliged to supply food and drink vouchers although, in fairness to them, most of them do. It is the passenger's responsibility to take out a holiday insurance to cover such eventualities.

Missing luggage

I have mentioned this subject elsewhere in the book but, briefly, the airline is responsible for delivering your luggage safely and will usually do something to help immediately. You may claim up to £850 in compensation for lost luggage, unless, of course, you are a petulant, egocentric pop star when it seems you are at liberty to claim the earth.

Surcharges

Regulations dictate that no price increases are allowed within thirty days of departure, and prior to that they can only be increased due to rises in taxes, exchange rates, airport charges, or a rise in fuel prices or other transportation costs, which seemingly can mean anything the operators want it to.

Overbooking

Although not a problem in the UK this does arise many times at overseas airports, where, in places like Nigeria, you just have to grin and bear it. In the UK or any other EU country, you can apply for immediate compensation if you find yourself "bumped off" a flight for which you have a confirmed reservation and have booked in on time. The compensation depends on the length of the flight, £100 for a flight up to 2,175 miles, and £200 for longer flights. These amounts will be adjusted if you are offered alternative flights within a short space of time. You claim through your tour operator. This only applies to package holidays *not* to charter flights.

In the late sixties, before the Saudi royal family had purchased their own personal aircraft, it was quite common for one of them to commandeer one of the Saudair fleet to fly him somewhere at a moment's notice. They thought nothing of leaving two hundred passengers stranded at the airport with no idea of when the next aircraft would arrive. And there certainly was no compensation.

Tour operator goes bust

This should not be a problem if you have taken the advice offered earlier and booked through a travel agency bonded with ABTA, ATOL, or AITO. You can doubly protect yourself by paying for your holiday with a credit card.

Hotel complaints

This is probably the commonest problem that tourists encounter, but if you take the appropriate action you should receive satisfaction at the end of the day. We are all familiar with finding building or renovation work still being carried out on arrival at the hotel that looked ideal in the brochure. Or finding the "secluded beach with golden sands" is only secluded because it is the outfall for the local sewerage system. If you feel, and can prove with photographs taken on your holiday, that the hotel was misrepresented then you can take action against the tour operator under the 1968 Trade Descriptions Act.

Every travel agent should have a copy of the *"Gazetteer"* which will give you a true description of what you are likely to find at your destination, as opposed to what the tour operator's brochure tells you awaits you. Ask to see it when you book your holiday, it could prevent a lot of misery.

Tour operators can no longer claim that problems abroad are

someone else's responsibility. The 1992 Package Travel Regulations state that they can be held liable in a British court for any incompetence on the part of their foreign associates.

Always take the holiday brochure with you on holiday so that you know what you have paid for and what you are entitled to. Complain to your tour operator at the first opportunity. It is not much use staying at the hotel for two weeks and then complaining on your return to the UK. Within twenty-eight days of your return home write a letter of complaint to the Customer Services Department at the tour operator's head office. If you receive no satisfaction take your evidence, as much as possible, to your local trading standards officer. Video footage is best especially if your complaint concerns noise. If you have no video camera it is possible to record excessive noise on a cassette. Remember to keep receipts of any extra expenses you incur.

If you and other clients at the hotel go down with food poisoning or some other malady, be sure to make notes, take photographs of evidence of bad practices, exchange telephone numbers and addresses and, on returning home, use only one firm of solicitors who have experience in this field. As a group you will have more clout than as individuals.

Do not believe that everything in small print on the booking form is sacrosanct. Many clauses in these contracts have been successfully challenged in the Small Claims Courts.

Alternatively, you can always contact one of the television consumer programmes that seem to delight in embarrassing the tourist industry.

Airsmiles 4
"How often do aircraft of this type crash?" enquired the nervous passenger of the flight attendant.

"Usually only once," came the reply.

CHAPTER FIVE

Local Customs and Culture

Offensive words

Culture is one of the things that distinguishes man from animals. It is also more important than colour when distinguishing one race from another, as is abundantly clear in India. The *Rajputs* (high castes) will not even drink from the same cups as the *Harijan* (untouchables) in the village tea houses, where separate crockery is kept for their use. The *Harijan* are not allowed to use the bucket at the well and must wait for a person of high caste to provide the water for them.

The colours worn, jewellery, the tying of the turban, even the shape of one's moustache are all used to differentiate between the various cultures in India where the caste system reigns supreme.

The more one travels the more one has to be careful of inadvertently offending people by doing or saying something that, although perfectly acceptable back home, could cause great offence in a foreign country. I met a woman once who had used the Welsh phrase for dirty pig in Ankara and was horrified to find it meant something equally rude in Turkish. One only has to think of the Duke of Edinburgh to realise how easy it is to offend people overseas. He has manged to do it on every continent with the exception of Antartica, and that's only because he has probably never been there.

Most spoken mistakes are more comical than offensive, as was the case when President Kennedy attempted to inform the people of Berlin that he was one of them. By inserting the word *ein* into the statement *"Ich bin ein Berliner"* he informed the world that he was a current cake! Whilst on the subject of the German language, the word *baiser* means a meringue in Austria and a kiss in Germany, so be careful in the cakeshop. One also has to be careful when using the word *"prost";* it may mean "cheers" in Scandanavia, but means "stupid" in Rumania. If you feel like sleeping on a KLM flight it is inadvisable to tell the

88

stewardess you would like a *kip* — it translates to chicken in Dutch. Equally simple mistakes can be made in France where the word *tampon* is a date stamp as used in libraries. This could prove to be uncomfortable as well as embarrassing.

The expression *voce me deixou embaracada* means "You have embarrassed me" in Portugal, but in Spain, just over the border, it translates as "You have made me pregnant", which could be equally embarrassing.

The simple word *vest* is an undergarment in the UK, a waistcoat in the United States, and a jacket in France.

Even accomplished linguists can make mistakes; a UK politician used the phrase "out of sight, out of mind" at a recent European Parliament meeting. It was translated as "invisible maniac".

I speak French fairly well but not having faith in my own ability cost me over £100 a short while ago. I pulled on to a car park in Hazebrouck, in the north of France, late one Sunday night. Having read the instructions I put the necessary amount of euros into the machine and walked off. As I was leaving the car park a sign caught my eye, *Stationment interdit Lundi.*

"Parking forbidden Monday?" I asked myself. No, it cannot be right. Why have a car park closed on a Monday? It didn't make sense.

I returned the following morning to find a busy market in full swing. My car had been carried off at the crack of dawn.

89

Not only did it take a whole morning traipsing around the local police station and Gendarmerie, filling in forms and paying fines, a photograph of my vehicle being carried away made the front page of the *Voix De Nord,* the local paper.

In France if you are informed that you are being sent to Limoges do not expect to be buying porcelain, it is the equivalent of being sent to Coventry in the UK!

On one contract I was involved with in Libya an American company had to change its name from KESCO as this had a very unfortunate translation into Arabic, referring to part of the female anatomy. Also if an Arab has a sore throat it is not advisable to tell him to suck a Zube, this being the male equivalent of the aforementioned female part.

In Arabic, the words for an apple and an ashtray sound exactly the same to the untrained ear. Many a smoker requested a *tuffiya* and ended up with an unwanted Cox's Pippin!

For reasons that I have never been able to discover, Oil of Ulay is now sold as Oil of Olay in the UK but is still sold as Oil of Ulay in various parts of the world. Other well known brand names also change as they travel. Why I want to know, was a Marathon chocolate bar renamed Snickers? Of the two I think Snickers sounds more offensive.

The daftest of complaints that I heard of was that Coca-Cola viewed upside down means something offensive in Arabic! Who the Hell stands on their head to look at advertisements? The Jewish community in the USA claimed that Marlboro says "orrible jew" when viewed upside down. The mind boggles.

The reason that Colgate may not be the most popular toothpaste in Spain and its ex-colonies is that *colgate* translates as "go hang yourself" in Spanish. A well-known hair product company tried to persuade the Germans to buy the"Mist Stick" curling iron without realising the word "mist" is the slang word for "manure" in Germany. It was not their most successful line ever. And a scooter hiring establishment in Corfu named Acharavi Kamikaze did not do a booming trade with Japanese tourists.

Not even names are safe. The English pronunciation of Paul can cause raised eyebrows in Germany or Austria. I worked for a while with a chap from Denmark whose name was Knut. I called him "nut" for a week before I discovered he was actually "Canute". I never did pluck up enough courage to call an Egyptian worker Fathi by name. However I pronounced it, it seemed equally offensive.

The Germans take the cake when it comes to offensive names. Kotze (vomit) and Morder (murderer), and even Hitler are still to be found there. Even more common are Dreckmann (filthman), Fett (fat),

Faul (lazy), Dumm (stupid), and Schwein (pig).

The Turks still harbour a militaristic tradition in naming their children. It is not unusual to find a clerk in a bank or a checkout assistant with the glorious name of Attila or Genghis, whereas we in the UK are different. When did you last hear of someone naming their child Horatio, or even Winston?

The Hindus probably have the strangest ritual for naming a baby. They resist giving the child a name for the first few months, then the whole family gathers together each bringing along a name they have chosen. Every person lights an oil lamp at the same time then they sit and feast and generally have a good time until all the lamps have burnt out. The owner of the lamp that burned the longest gets to name the child. It prevents any squabbles in the family as they believe that God has a hand in the procedure.

There are also occasions when a word or words can look quite innocuous when written but turn out to be quite the opposite when spoken. There was a case of a racehorse being registered in New Zealand with the name "Four Quenelle". The official keeper-of-the-stud thought nothing of it until he heard a commentary of a race it was running in. It was very swiftly rechristened.

While on the subject of New Zealand, if, while there, you are invited to a party and told to "bring a plate", it doesn't mean the hostess is short of crockery. You are expected to bring a plate of food to share around. After all, if invited to "bring a bottle", you would not turn up with an empty one would you?

The simple sneeze is regarded completely differently in some parts of the world. For the Chinese, to sneeze on New Year's Eve means bad luck for the whole year. To the Jews, to sneeze during prayer is considered a pleasure sent from God. Some Welshmen think that sneezing at certain times is unlucky. While shaving with a cut-throat razor?

The Bushmen of the Kalahari Desert have no sense of ownership. Everything is considered communial property and shared. It is not too much of a problem if it's just your cigarettes they help themselves to, but it can be a bit of a shock to turn round and find that one of them has helped himself to your safari jacket!

Offensive actions

No-one can be expected to be word perfect in every language, (there are six thousand different languages in use around the world), so slips of the tongue are to be expected. The thing to beware of is offending by particular actions that can well be avoided by a little prior investigation. No sensible businessman now attempts to take alcohol into Saudi Arabia, although how many know that replicas of any living creature cause offence to devout Muslims? Or that Christmas trees will be confiscated? One will find no modern statues in a lot of Middle East countries and in several where the Romans left examples of their art, as at Leptis Magna in Libya, many of the female statues are minus their breasts, and faces of both sexes have been mutilated.

Many Americans make the mistake of attempting to bring jade carvings from the Far East into Saudi Arabia only to have them confiscated by Customs officials. Another Muslim tradition is to incorporate a fault into a new building, for example leaving out one brick, because it is written that only Allah can do perfect works. Some cynics say this tradition carries over to everything the Arabs attempt, not only building. Construction workers are warned to be careful when criticising shoddy workmanship; it may be deliberate.

During Ramadan Muslims must refrain from "all pleasures of the flesh" during the hours of daylight. This includes food and drink with the exception of a little water to wash the mouth. Obviously, the sick and very young are excluded but all able-bodied followers of Islam are expected to conform. It is then common courtesy not to eat, drink, and smoke in the company of Arabs who are abstaining. It must be difficult enough to go without food and drink for twelve hours without having some *infidel* stuffing his face with a greasy burger right under your nose.

The "V" sign can signify victory or peace in some countries but is definitely meant to be offensive in the UK. How many people realise it dates back to the 15th century?, to 1415 in fact. The French used to disable English archers taken prisoner by removing the middle and forefinger. After the battle of Agincourt, or Azincourt if you are French, when celebrating an overwhelming victory, the English soldiers gloated over the enemy by holding up their hands with the first two fingers upright to show both fingers intact.

The Nigerians curse one another by pointing the hand with all fingers extended (the five finger salute), whereas in other parts of Africa it is just the outside fingers raised with the two middle fingers folded down (hook horns).

The British and Americans beckon the waiter with the index finger raised, on the continent this usually results in another drink being brought, and in Japan is considered downright rude. In Japan it is also impolite to talk to someone with your hands in your pockets.

The common stop sign of extending one hand, palm forward is an insulting gesture in some West African countries.

The great British tradition of going on strike (also very popular in France!), is definitely frowned upon in a lot of overseas countries. When a crowd of Brits employed at Dhahran Airport went on a sit-in strike in the canteen some years ago, the Saudis ringed the building with tanks and threatened to open fire if the men did not report back to work immediately. By all accounts work was swiftly resumed.

Another thing to beware of in Muslim countries is eating with the left hand. This hand is kept exclusively for performing matters of hygiene. When attending formal dinners, known affectionately as "mutton grabs", one is advised to sit on the left hand to avoid its inadvertent use. This is not as ridiculous as it sounds because one will be sat on the floor anyway as chairs and tables are conspicuously absent on these occasions. The meat, rice, and fruit are piled high on huge platters placed in the centre of the carpet and everyone sits around and dives in. The old hands pair off one each side of the dish and act as a team when it comes to breaking off chicken legs or wrestling with half an antelope.

However, even the most wary can come unstuck. I stood next to a Senior Air Traffic Controller at Khamis Mushait on one occasion, and as he shook hands with the Crown Prince on his departure, the Prince and I were sprayed with rice that the controller had scooped unknowingly into his shirt sleeve while helping himself to the delicacies on offer.

Whilst on the subject of royalty, I was once invited to a disco at the Royal Palace in Rabat, Morocco. My companion was a local woman who ran her own PR company. On arriving at the palace she introduced me to a string of people including army officers, local ministers, and diplomats from a variety of embassies. After a while it became routine, a quick handshake and a 'pleased to meet you'. At one point we stopped at a table where a dumpy woman dressed very casually in a loose black jumper and matching baggy trousers was sitting. I performed the ritual handshake and 'pleased to meet you' and turned to find my companion looking aghast. She then informed me that I had just insulted the King's sister! I was supposed to kiss her hand not shake it.

Not wishing to end my days in an Arab dungeon I hastily returned, kissed the proffered hand, and apologised profusely explaining that I was an Englishman who had just been introduced to more people than I could count. She was very gracious and later, during a violent thunderstorm, I accompanied her to the stables to check on her many horses.

Maybe it's because I was born in London, but I have a distinct phobia where any animal bigger than a dog is concerned. I will walk around a field rather than enter it if cows are present. Horses I especially do not like. The Arab stallions in Princess Asma's stable all realised this immediately. She was highly amused as I walked strictly down the centre of the stable keeping every horse equidistant from me. Each horse in turn greeted me with laid back ears, rolling eyes, and flared nostrils.

In France it is considered discourteous to arrive on time at a social event such as a cocktail party or when invited to someone's home for a meal. The host expects the guests to be between ten and thirty minutes late. However, business meetings are conducted on time. On the subject of time, be careful in northern Europe; when a Norwegian or German states "half nine" he means half an hour before nine, i.e. half past eight. Other countries do the same so stick to the twenty-four hour clock when making appointments.

Incidently, the Asians have a proverb "Lateness is the theft of time" so it pays to be punctual when dealing in the orient.

When in a meeting in Japan and presented with a business card do not immediately put it into your pocket or briefcase as this is taken as an indication that the meeting is over. Leave the card on view on the table until taking your leave. If presented with a card at a casual meeting keep it in your hand until you have said goodbye. Courtesy is extremely important when dealing with the Japanese and the Arabs so a little time, or money, spent getting clued up on local customs before travelling to do business will not go amiss.

If you are fortunate enough to be invited to a Japanese household be very careful when using the bathroom. Taking a bath is a ritual in Japan. One is expected to shower first and then, when clean, to enter a scalding hot bath to relax for as long as you wish. Do not pull the plug on leaving as the water will be utilised by all the menbers of the family. You know you have been accepted by the family when they cease waiting for you to take the first bath.

Incidently, if while driving in Japan you see a group of children standing by the roadside waving, they are not greeting you. It is the local way of requesting drivers to stop to allow them to cross.

If invited to dine with a Chinese family do not clear the plate as you are then insinuating that you were not given enough. You will find your plate replenished until you leave something.

It is also wise to remember that just about every other country on earth is more nationalistic than the English. What other country does not celebrate its national day? How many Englishmen even know when St George's Day is? To a lesser extent the whole of Britain is guilty of this lack of national pride; where else would one find the national flag turned into a pair of underpants or a minidress for a pop star? However, I do believe the Greeks have gone overboard somewhat having a national anthem with 158 verses. If they played the whole thing before a football match we would have the final whistle before the kick-off!

I have always made a point of respecting the national pride of whatever country I have found myself in, especially in Africa where so many of the new nations have recently fought bitter wars for their independance. Airbus Industries picked up a very lucrative contract for new aircraft from Air Zimbabwe because their rivals, Boeing, sent their demonstration aircraft into Harare Airport gloriously festooned with the flag of Southern Rhodesia, much to the chagrin of President Robert Mugabe.

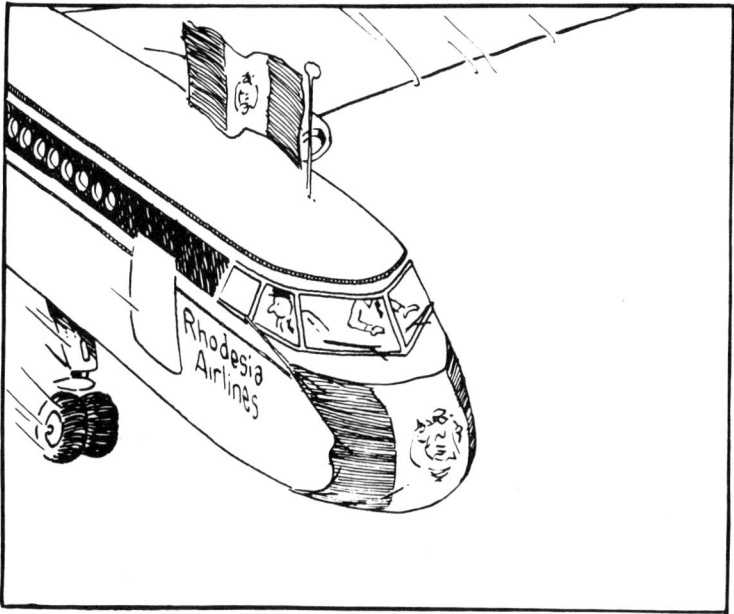

The most unorthodox meeting I ever attended was with the Nigerian Air Force in Lagos. High ranking officers, myself, and our local agent were sitting around a large table in a very impressive conference room when the door suddenly opened and two airmen marched in carrying crates of Guinness and plates of chips. In five minutes the meeting degenerated into a drunken party!

In countries such as Spain and Italy which are predominantly Roman Catholic, women are expected to cover their heads when entering religious buildings. In Islamic countries it is forbidden for anyone not of the Muslim faith to enter a mosque.

Shortly after first arriving in Saudi Arabia in 1969 I remember going to the *souk* to buy a few items to brighten up my living quarters. I bought a nice red patterned cloth for a small table beside my bed. The following day Gamullah, the teaboy, had a fit when he saw it. He was shaking his head saying "Lah, lah" (no, no), but I had no idea what he was going on about. Later, one of the Saudi students explained that my "tablecloth" was the headscarf of the elite Saudi Guard, the King's own regiment. I quickly removed it from sight. It just went to show just how easy it is to innocently upset people.

Be very careful when taking photographs overseas, especially around military sites and airfields. Many foreign governments are very sensitive about their military hardware, as some aeroplane spotters found out recently in Greece.

In most African and Asian countries it is advisable to ask permission before photographing strangers. Some countries, such as Nepal, actively discourage tourists from photographing the locals.

Acceptable dress

Living as I do in a holiday resort in Devon I am quite accustomed to visitors wandering around the place dressed in anything they feel comfortable in. For the most part it does not affect me, I have no objection to men and women lying on the beach exposing themselves to the sun's rays. I do, however, object to being confronted by sweating, hairy armpits, male or female, while I am sitting at the bar in the pub. Thankfully, the landlord of my local feels as I do, and insists on customers covering up if they wish to be served.

In many places overseas the local authorities are not as liberal as those in the UK so a little discretion may prevent embarrassment, or worse. After all, would anyone in his right mind walk into a North London pub on a Saturday night wearing a Manchester United football shirt?

Women have to be particulary careful how they dress in many Muslim countries, especially Saudi Arabia and Iran. Arms are expected to be covered to the wrists, and legs to the ankles, and as the temperature can reach 120 degrees Fahrenheit this is not the most comfortable way to dress. Young Arab women are no different to their European sisters and like to dress fashionably when abroad but have to abide by a strict dress code when returning home to Saudi Arabia. An hour before the aircraft touches down at Dhahran, Riyadh, or Jeddah there is a constant stream of miniskirted young ladies disappearing into the toilets to reappear minutes later clad from head to foot in black robes (the *chador*) and shuffling down the aisle like so many animated Guinness bottles.

Many Saudi women are expected to walk a few paces behind their husbands, and it is not uncommon to see four wives piled into the back of a truck with the goats while the husband and children sit inside the vehicle enjoying the comfort of air conditioning.

In the late sixties long haired expatriates would find themselves escorted to the nearest barbershop by the *mutawaeen* during the month of Ramadan for a most unfashionable haircut, though things were a lot more relaxed the last time I was in the country. As previously mentioned, during Ramadan, when devout Muslims abstain from all pleasures of the flesh during the hours of daylight, it is considered good manners if non-Muslims refrain from eating or smoking in their presence.

I have known an Arab to turn his deckchair away from the swimming pool during Ramadan as he did not wish to have the pleasure of seeing young ladies in bathing costumes. This seems to me to be taking things to extremes.

Shorts are certainly frowned upon in countries such as Saudi Arabia and Kuwait, (and also in Rome), and banks in Riyadh have been known to turn away male customers wearing them. In fact, it was not so many years ago when a female customer was unheard of in a Saudi bank. A woman appearing as a presenter on TV with her face uncovered risked being found in an alley with her throat cut.

I have always found the wearing of the *yashmak* and *hijab* puzzling. Any normal man, surely, is happy to walk along with a beautiful woman on his arm, and the more envious glances he attracts the better he likes it. Some Arab men, however, insist on their wives wearing a face mask. We are led to believe that this is because she is so lovely he wants to keep her all to himself. On the odd occasion I have seen one of these gorgeous apparitions reveal herself I have come to the conclusion the husband is doing us all a favour, because she has invariably been as ugly as sin. I believe it more likely that the mask was invented in the times when smallpox was prevalent and the device was to hide the ravages of this disease.

Incidently, nowhere does the Koran state that women should cover themselves in this way, it only says that women should dress modestly, i.e. not walk around bare breasted as had been the fashion at the time the holy book was written. Nor does the Koran advocate the slaying of non believers. In fact, it states on two separate occasions that "Jews and Christians and whoever believes in God and does what is right shall have nothing to fear or regret". As in every religion unscrupulous people have translated the texts to suit their own ends.

At the time of writing women are still not officially allowed to drive in Saudi Arabia or Kuwait, although, since the Gulf conflict, a few indigenous feminists have risked prosecution by following the example set by military females.

Humour

Humour is something to be very careful of when travelling. Whoever said "laugh and the world laughs with you" had certainly not worked in Saudi Arabia. I once, in an unguarded moment, jokingly remarked that if I did not get my ticket home on time I would sabotage the radar equipment. The following morning I was arrested in the workshop, driven miles into the desert to a military camp, confronted by an army colonel, and threatened with execution. I had known the colonel for years, since he had been a lieutenant in fact, but did not doubt for one moment that he would have carried out his threat if he had really considered my remark to be serious.

A British Section Leader I worked with was frustrated when a group of Saudi technicians, whose minds were on a forthcoming trip to Bangkok rather than the lesson in hand, persisted in behaving in an unruly manner in the classroom. He lobbed a banana into the middle of them saying "If you wish to act like monkeys you can eat like them." He was home almost as fast as he could pack. The Saudis do not like to be called monkeys.

On the subject of bananas, Dr Canaan Banana, a former President of Zimbabwe, was so fed up with hearing fun being poked at his name that he banned all jokes about himself. It just made the telling of the jokes that much funnier.

Arabs take any form of insult very seriously. At Riyadh on one occasion I was involved in the installation of navigation aids at the airport. Being a military establishment it was necessary to produce identity cards on entry, but once the guards became familiar with our vehicles we were admitted with just a cursory glance. All of us that is, with the exception of a young man working with a team of aerial erectors.

I think most riggers will forgive me if I describe them as a rough and ready lot. It is a physically demanding task and only the toughest make it a career. The young man in question was the son of the firm's Managing Director and had been sent to Saudi Arabia for experience. He was aged twenty or thereabouts but looked much younger. He also had a mass of blond curls. There was no doubt he stood out from the rest of the British contingent who, for the most part, were like myself, time served ex-regular armed forces technicians.

The Saudi guards were fascinated by him and every time he approached a security gate his vehicle was stopped. Hook nosed soldiers would leer at him and stroke his arms much to the amusement of the rest of us, and to his intense embarrassment. One day his patience snapped and as an especially evil-looking character approached his vehicle he revved up, and blowing a loud raspberry roared off in a cloud of dust. The result of his outburst was that he was charged with insulting the King!

This amazing conclusion had been reached because the guard was in uniform and the cap badge is the royal emblem. Saudi logic has to be experienced to be believed. The poor chap had to make a public apology to an assembly of security guards and their officers in order to save his father's contract.

Treatment of animals

Where animals are concerned no other country seems to have the dotty devotion that is typical of most pet owners in Britain. Most Arabs seem to be feelingless and I have seen decrepid old donkeys beaten almost senseless hauling loads that two carthorses would be hard pushed to contend with. Sheep and goats were slaughtered daily by having their throats cut outside the dining hall at Khamis Mushait Airbase. This was done with a small knife while other animals stood by and awaited their turn.

I have had to restrain British technicians, and myself, when we have seen Saudi young men place a lighted cigarette end into a pet cat's ear, or hurl stones at birds we have encouraged to frequent the gardens we built in the desert.

On one occasion I was surprised to see a young Arab girl with a pet jerboa as animals in the Middle East are generally kept only to eat or work. Closer inspection revealed that both its back legs had been broken to prevent it escaping. It was obviously destined for the pot.

Cruelty to animals is by no way restricted to Asia. There are some appalling zoos around the world in supposedly civilised countries, and does anyone in their right mind believe that tigers and lions perform in circuses because they want to amuse people? Bull fighting is totally accepted by the indigenous population of Spain and yet causes the hackles to rise of 90% of British tourists who visit the country. The French, in typical sporting fashion, blast thousands of migrating birds out of the air every year, and the Italians race horses headlong around cobbled streets with the inevitable consequences. Across the Atlantic, the Americans have spent the last two hundred years decimating the wildlife of the United States to such an extent that they now seem to be reduced to shooting one another to satisfy their lust for killing.

Local customs
While working with the Koreans on the Great Manmade River Project in Libya it took some while to get used to being called by my surname. It seems that in Korea only family members and intimate friends are addressed by their Christian names, or non Christian names as the case may be.

Another thing that surprised me about the Koreans was the fact that many of them returned from a trip home with their hair dyed black and yet made no attempt to dye it when the grey hair started to show through again whilst in Libya. I eventually discovered that at home it was considered an insult to one's parents to have grey hair whilst the father was still alive. I knew one engineer whose father was ninety-two but he was still expected to dye his hair whenever he went home, although he was near pension age himself.

Koreans also think that blowing one's nose into a handkerchief and then pocketing the object and its contents is a dirty habit, but they think nothing of using the office wastepaper bin as a spitoon. And the noises they make clearing their throats has to be heard to be believed.

Another phenomenon I witnessed whilst working with the Koreans was the fruit break in the afternoon. At two o'clock precisely someone would arrive in the office with a tray of water melon, grapes, or other fruit and everyone would adjourn to a communal table and proceed to tuck in. I have no idea whether this event is commonplace in Korea or just peculiar to the company I worked for, but it certainly made a pleasant change from endless cups of tea.

The letter "Q" does not exist in many foreign languages, which may explain why so many foreigners have no idea what a queue is. African and Arab women never queue. Whether you are waiting for a bus or waiting to be treated for an emergency in a casualty ward, you can bet your boots if you are white and male that some female will barge in front of you. There is no point in making a fuss as no-one will take a blind bit of notice.

One very strange custom I came across was in the Biafran area of Nigeria. Ibo men do not make love to their wives whilst the woman is breast-feeding a baby, which can be for as long as two years. However, during this time it is perfectly acceptable for him to sleep with other women.

If travelling to Nigeria you must be prepared to come in contact with the custom of "dash". This is purely and simply a euphanism for bribery. Nothing in the country operates unless *dash* is paid. To get a seat on an aircraft, even if holding an OK ticket, one will have to *dash* the person at the check-in counter. To collect mail or a parcel from the post office it is necessary to *dash* the counter clerk, and to get a signature on a multi-million dollar contract one is expected to *dash* a minister. It is pointless to argue as the system is now a way of life in the country. Similar goings-on are to be found in many other countries but nowhere so blatantly as in Nigeria.

One thing to be aware of in Africa is the use of the words "brother" and "sister". This term can be applied to anyone from the same town or village as the speaker. When referring to a family member an African will usually say something like "brother, same father" which means his father had more than one wife and the person referred had a different mother. For a full brother or sister he will say "same father, same mother".

A thing that has always surprised me is the way that film makers always depict the Africans as singing happily as they lug huge crates through the jungle, or haul boats half the size of the *Queen Mary* up the Niger. In all my thirty years of working on the dark continent from Morocco to Lesotho, from Nigeria to Kenya, I can never recall hearing a group of natives singing except on a stage. And as for "natural rhythm" it just does not exist. The first time I went into the Can-Can Club at Apapa in Lagos and saw the crowd on the dance floor, I thought the band's amplifiers had shorted to earth and everyone was being electrocuted. They were twitching and jumping about completely oblivious to the tune being played.

Americans are the only race I know who make no effort to assimilate any other culture. Wherever they go in the world the Americans export their own culture, or rather lack of it. When I worked for ARAMCO at Ras Tanura in Saudi Arabia, the American employees had their own compound complete with US style shops, schools with imported teachers, MacDonalds, and a tenpin bowling alley. They even had a miniature Coney Island for the children.

One thing that does surprise Europeans travelling to Africa and Asia is the apparent disrespect for the dead. In many African countries victims of road accidents are often left lying in the road to be trundled over by subsequent heavy lorries until they become indistinguishable from the tarmac. In Lagos, a *nightwatch,* who was killed by robbers, was left lying in the front garden for three days until eventually being carted off by the refuse wagon.

In Riyadh, in 1971, a man was knocked down and killed in a road accident outside the Airport Hotel just before I left for work at eight o'clock in the morning. When I returned to the hotel at six o'clock in the evening he was still lying at the kerbside, but now minus his shoes.

In many cases this callous regard of the dead is simply due to the fact that the victims are itinerant workers and no-one knows where they come from or who the relatives are.

I know for a fact that in Nigeria the death of a relative is taken very seriously. A son is expected to spend all his savings, and even go into debt, to ensure his father has a proper send-off. I have known a wake to last as long as a week for a particularly respected father.

Tradition in Nigeria states that when a Chief or Oba dies there must be seven heads buried with the body to look after his needs in the next world. Modern Nigerians claim that this custom is no longer adhered to, but I know when the Chief died in Orabum village, where I was living at the time, there were an unusual amount of "road accidents" (seven in all) the following week.

The Islamic religion states that a man should give a percentage of his earnings to the poor, I believe 10% but am not certain of this. It's irrelevent anyway, because as far as I can see no Arab abides by this philosophy. All it achieves is to encourage begging. In all Muslim countries an expat can expect to be pestered by beggars whenever he is on the streets. Even in fabulously rich countries like Saudi Arabia beggars abound. Nigeria and Bangladesh were the worst two countries as far as I was concerned especially on the ferries where one was trapped at the mercy of every scrounger on board. By the time one drove off at the other side the car windows would be covered in greasy fingerprints, babies' dribble, and other unmentionable material. Be warned, giving a donation may rid you of one beggar but will attract a dozen or so more.

Thumbnail sketches of other travellers

As travelling the globe is no longer the prerogative of the British as it was in the days of the first Queen Elizabeth, you must be prepared to meet tourists from other parts of the world as you go from place to place. I hope the following brief descriptions will prepare you for their little idiosyncracies.

Americans

The typical American will arrive on holiday, or rather vacation, attired in a loud, short-sleeved shirt which hangs like a maternity smock. When not wearing "Bermudas" (a compromise between shorts and long trousers), he will wear slacks held up with a belt sporting a huge buckle usually depicting a bull's head or something equally macho.

A married couple will normally be accompanied by an overweight son and an oversexed daughter who delights in pawing her boyfriend in public. Whereas the parents usually wear shorts that reach to the knees, the kids sport slashed-down jeans that hardly cover their private parts.

The Americans are very boisterous and even when eating are not known to be silent. Most of them have perfected the art of talking while eating or smoking, seemingly without the necessity of pausing for breath. The whole family will be inclined to speak loudly and the women will find everything "cute"; even the exhibits in the Chamber of Horrors. The children have never been taught to sit, they either prowl about inspecting everything in sight or sprawl all over the furniture.

Americans, for all their apparent affluence, are surprisingly penny pinching and inspect every invoice thoroughly. Quite paradoxically, they are very generous tippers

Japanese

The Japanese always travel in shoals weighed down with an abundance of photographic and video equipment. They are invariably tightly packed with no stragglers, probably a habit learned in the jungles of Asia when the last man was likely to get picked off. The majority wear sparkling clean, gold rimmed glasses usually with very thick lenses.

The women follow meekly behind their menfolk and the young ones are invariably rather beautiful. Both sexes are always immaculately attired and speak excellent English. They have an unhealthy regard of physical fitness and can often be seen collectively carrying out strenuous routines on the hotel lawn at daybreak.

The Japanese have impeccable manners and will smile and greet every guest as he arrives in the hotel dining room and have even been known to stand *en masse* for the arrival of someone they consider important. They are delicate eaters and the more varied the menu the more they prefer it. They pay graciously but tips are inclined to be proportional to their physical characteristics.

Everything in the western world is a constant source of wonder to them and even woodworm in old furniture is greeted with "aah sos" of amazement.

French

Many of the French seem to take an instant aversion to we Brits and rudely refer to us as "ros bif" — an allusion to the fact that we are inclined to resemble rarely done beef on exposure to the sun. In Calais I was once warned by a French woman to leave my British registered car close to the exit where the car park attendant could keep an eye on it. It seems that some of the locals are not too pleased with all the Brits invading the area to purchase cheap alcohol and tobacco. However, I have lived in France on many occasions and have made very good friends there.

The French are very wary of British influence, so much so that the government passed an act banning the use of English words in daily speech. Even so, they still have no French word for television and "le weekend" is still widely used.

A lot of Frenchmen stink of awful tobacco and garlic, and constantly appear with two days' growth of stubble around the face. Despite these obvious drawbacks in appearance and aroma, every Frenchman insists on attempting to be "charmant". On the other hand, French women invariably smell of expensive perfume (some kind of defense mechanism against their male compatriots?), and are probably the best dressed women in the world.

The French take their eating extremely seriously and meals are usually conducted in absolute silence; unless the waiter inadvertently brings a bottle of South African wine. They do, however, eat the most peculiar things. The menu sometimes reads like the cast list from a David Attenborough documentary with snails, frogs, octopus, and squid all making an appearance.

Every Frenchman in Paris seems to think he is a formula one racing driver and the changing of traffic lights from red to green is like the start of the Indianapolis 500. He will roar away from the lights with tyres screaming and clutch burning. Thankfully, elsewhere in France they drive very differently but any British car is fair game and a Citroen 2CV6 will think nothing of trying to beat a Jaguar XJ12 down the autoroute.

The French tip often but not overgenerously.

Germans

The German traveller has one claim to fame; he is even more outrageously dressed than an American. Hideous checked materials appear compulsory wear for both sexes. Shirts, shorts, slacks, and even hats, in an explosion of colours seem intentionly designed to assault the eyes of any innocent beholder. On the beach there is a continual contest between Germans to see who can cram the largest *frau* into the smallest bikini; not a sight for the faint hearted!

Germans, like their French neighbours, also stink of awful cigarettes and even worse cigars. When eating or talking the Germans are extremely loud and a game of whist that they play sounds like a Saturday night in Murphy's bar as each card is thumped down on the table top with increasing vigour until the trick is won by the last man playing a card with such ferocity that the beer glasses leap three inches into the air. It is certainly nothing like the whist played in the church hall.

No matter at what unearthly hour the remainder of the guests arise in the morning they will find the Germans already firmly ensconced in all the most desirable places around the swimming pool.

A German will always be last to leave the bar at night. This is not only to try to prove that he can outdrink everyone else, but also so that he can check the list of early calls at reception and then book one earlier than anyone else, thereby ensuring he will be first at the pool to grab the best places for himself and his fellow countrymen.

The Germans will always attempt to outdrink the British, but, when losing, will resort to their well known "secret weapon" strategy and introduce schnapps. It tastes like nitroglycerine and has the same effect on reaching the brain.

The Germans can actually eat even more than the Americans and also use the fork as a shovel to get the food into themselves. After a full three course meal a German will easily devour a slice of Black Forest gateau half the size of a wedding cake.

They drive fast and efficiently but are not prone to giving away to other drivers, pushbikes or pedestrians. Where tipping is concerned they stick rigidly to the rules; if service charge is included, no tip, otherwise it is 10% exactly.

Italians

The Italian travelling family usually consists of Mama and Papa plus three or four children, the youngest of which will be a babe in arms and the eldest a teenage daughter in the first bloom of womanhood. Mother will spend the whole time fussing over the *bambino* while father will spend his time frantically protecting his daughter. Any male is considered a threat and this includes the seventy-year-old night porter at the hotel. Any waiter daring to stand too close to the girl is stared at malevolently by Papa while he slices the meat on his plate with meaningful gestures. While the parents are in attendance the daughter is innocence itself, but whenever unchaperoned for a moment will flirt outrageously with any man present.

The Italians like their meat marinaded in wine and exoctic herbs and will eat mountains of pasta especially if accompanied by copious quantities of chianti and a side salad dripping in olive oil.

Italian drivers are very similar to their French neighbours having a tendancy to roar away from traffic lights and take on any British car they happen to come across. However, with cars such as the Alpha Romeo, Maseratti, and Ferrari they do have a distinct advantage over the French.

On the subject of tipping, the Italians are as generous as they can afford to be. Not hailing from the most affluent of countries they do not have money to throw away.

Arabs

Arabs vary from the fabulously rich Saudi Arabians to scruffy Syrians resembling refugees from Afghanistan, so I will confine my remarks to the ones most likely to be met as tourists, the Saudis.

It is most likely that the Arab man you meet overseas will be reeking of Chanel No 5 (they use it as aftershave), and is a Prince to boot. This is not as surprising as it sounds because, besides the King's sons, his brothers, uncles and all their sons are also Princes. At the last count it was almost two hundred.

The Arabs all claim to be devout Muslims and refrain from eating any meat from the pig; no gammon steaks, bacon, pork sausages and the like. However, many of them conveniently forget their religion when it comes to consuming vast quantities of whisky and letching after women.

On the subject of eating, remember that the Islamic religion allows food to be consumed only with the right hand. Do not be surprised if all the Arabs at the table suddenly get up and leave should another diner inadvertently help himself to a bread roll with his left hand. The Muslims use this hand exclusively for the carrying out of ablutions.

This brings us to another unusual custom; the Arabs use water not toilet paper at the end of a visit to the "smallest room", so be prepared and carry a few tissues with you if visiting the Middle East unless you are willing to go native and use the hosepipe provided.

Most Saudis are extraordinarily rich and tip accordingly. They drive as though they own the roads, and let's face it, in many places they probably do.

The Brit Abroad

Prior to publishing I asked a journalist friend of mine to run an eye over my manuscript as I valued his opinion. Among his many good suggestions was the one that, in all fairness, I should include a thumbnail sketch of the typical Brit abroad.

Simple, I thought, as I cast my mind back forty years to when, after leaving the Royal Air Force, I commenced travelling the world as a civilian.

Usually clad in clean, well-pressed short sleeve shirt with matching shorts or in a safari suit. Hair trimmed and neatly combed. Sun glasses, camera, and desert boots completed the ensemble.

I was able to converse politely with the locals having made an effort to learn a few words of the language wherever I was to be working.

I suddenly realised I was describing a being from a by-gone age!

From what I have gleaned from travel documentaries on the TV the present day Brit one is likely to meet overseas is far different.

Union Jack shorts or calf length Bermudas struggling to contain a huge beer belly are topped off with a sleeveless T-shirt bearing an advert for beer or an obscene logo.The feet are encased in black Doc Marten's or cheap flip-flops. In either case socks are superfluous. The head is usually shaved to display to full affect the battle scars picked up at football matches or on previous jaunts abroad.

Both ears contain an assortment of rings and crosses and around the neck hangs half a hundredweight of dubious gold-coloured metal. Other parts of the body also contain an assortment of metalwork. (How do these people get through security checks at airports?)

Arms, legs, torsos, and other delicate parts of the body are adorned with the tattooist's art, or lack of art in many cases. Said person can usually be found carrying a can of lager in one hand and a half-eaten kebab in the other.

Language skills amount to "If you can't speak bleedin' English, don't bovver to talk to me!"

All I can add is thank goodness we still have some members of the armed forces abroad proving we do still produce youngsters we can be proud of.

Airsmiles 5
During a fire in a high-rise building six men and a woman are snatched from the roof by a helicopter. As they hang suspended on a rope beneath the aircraft the pilot realises that the load is too much and that they will all be dragged down to their deaths. He informs them that one will have to let go.

No one can decide who it should be but finally the woman volunteers. She gives a heartrending speech saying she will sacrifice herself for the others because women are used to giving up their careers and all their time for their husbands and children.

When she finishes her speech all the men start clapping.

CHAPTER SIX

Recreation

Drinking abroad

Although I eventually settled on the title of "Recreation" for this chapter, having read it through I realise my recreational pursuits overseas seemed to have been rather limited and a new title of "BARS" seemed more appropriate. Also, having spent over thirty-five years *working* abroad it appears to me presumptive to give advice to people going abroad with probably the sole purpose of enjoying themselves, but I have included it with the hope that it may prevent others making a few mistakes that I have made.

My earliest memories of foreign drinking establishments are as a young airman in Germany in 1958. It seems nothing much has changed because even in those days we Brits had already earned ourselves a reputation for being unruly in drink. If one required to use the toilet faciliites in the village pub it was necessary to draw the key from old Mutti behind the bar, as the loo was kept permanently locked. She would make frequent excursions throughout the evening to check on the state of the plumbing. *"Die Schlussel bitte"* was the first German phrase learned by many a National Serviceman at Jever.

The Germans are serious beer drinkers. Besides the world renowned Oktoberfest they also have *shutzenfests* to celebrate the beginning of various shooting seasons, and *Rosenmontag* (Rose Monday), when married women leave off their wedding rings and have a night on the town. I have also heard it described as *Rasenmontag* (Mad Monday), which is a far more apt description of events as I recall them.

In Holland, however, the use of English is recommended. I made the mistake of assuming it would be more helpful to use German, the country is, after all, just over the border, but having had my beer almost thrown at me and my change deposited in the largest puddle on the counter I soon realised it was advantageous to let the proprietor know one is British as soon as possible. World War Two has definitely not been forgotten in Holland.

The ringing of the bell in a Dutch pub is not to be greeted with dismay. It is not the signal to down what's left in the glass and rush to grab a last drink before closing, as is the case in the UK. In Holland, the ringer of the bell is announcing his intention to buy the whole bar a drink. The ringer could be a prospective bridegroom, someone celebrating a birthday, or even a shrewd bar owner livening up proceedings on a cold, quiet winter's night. It's surprising how quickly the habit of ringing the bell catches on once it has started. Having had a couple of free drinks it takes a real brass neck to get up and leave without reciprocating.

In Holland on one occasion I was surprised when my wife and I were persistently presented with free drinks in a little bar in Vollendam. It was only with great difficulty that I eventually managed to pay for a round. Later in the evening the barman explained why we were being treated so generously. It appeared that while I had been visiting the toilet a customer had mistaken my wife for one of the prostitutes who usually frequented the place and tried to talk her into leaving with him.

Fortunately, not understanding a word of what he had said, she had assumed he was just being friendly. By the time I was informed what had happened I had consumed too many free drinks to know whether I should feel insulted or flattered.

In France while having a drink I have often thought I've strayed into the bar of the Starship Enterprise. The array of colours of drinks is amazing. It is strange to see grown men supping violet, blue, green, or yellow drinks. With what drink can anyone want to mix syrup of violets which is to be found in most French bars?

The French also have a bottled beer *Desperado* which contains tequila and another, *Adelscott,* which contains whisky. And where else but France would they drink strawberry flavoured beer or mix beer with Coca-Cola (a *mazout).* Ordinary drinks in France can have strange names too; *baby coq* is a whisky and coke.

If you are fortunate enough to find yourself in the vicinity of Toulouse around the end of September, there is a small town named Tarascon sur Ariege well worth a visit. At this time every year there is a livestock market, the Grande Foire Saint Michel, when the local farmers bring down for sale their animals from the high summer pastures in the Pyranees.

Many local farmers earn their entire annual income on this one day. To say the wine flows freely is an understatement, it gushes forth! Having collected money for their livestock the flush herdsmen wander from bar to bar greeting old friends and often buying rounds for the entire assembled clientele.

I met a bar owner in Hesdin, a small town not too far from Abbeville, who spoke excellent English and, on enquiring where he had obtained his proficiency in the language, he informed me that he had once been married to an English "barmaid in the sky". I do not think too many air stewardesses would be happy to hear themselves described as such.

Paying for drinks

The manner of paying for drinks varies greatly from place to place. In the UK we are accustomed to paying on receipt of goods but many countries allow one to settle up at the end of the session. The beer mat is often used as a running receipt with drinks ticked off around the edge and totalled up at the end. I am afraid the lager louts on the continent, not only British ones, will be responsible for the decline of this custom which is so open to abuse.

At some bars the drinks are actually paid for at the bar by the waitress and delivered to the table for a small extra charge. It only needs a couple of drinks to be erased from the beer mat for the poor girl to be working for nothing.

Some countries, especially Italy, charge more for drinks consumed at the table than at the bar even if there is not a waitress service. In France this is generally not the case.

In bars where the drinks are paid for at the end of the session it is advisable to get a receipt with every round. This way it is possible to check that you are only paying for drinks you are actually served, and the final bill will not come as too much of a shock.

In some drinking establishments in Switzerland they have a strap running around the inside of the bar. A customer's receipt is tucked away in front of him until the time for settling up. On one occasion I was drinking with a group of American engineers and the millionaire owner of the Dallas Cowboys football team. The conversation was good and the dumpy bottles of Swiss beer flowed freely, as did the occasional Scotch and vodka. I didn't take much notice as one by one everyone drifted away until I was left holding the fort and a huge pile of receipts. It was the most expensive round I have ever bought. There is a lot to be said for paying as one goes.

In the UK, and the rest of Europe as far as I know, one rarely, if ever, tips the barmen. An occasional drink is quite enough to guarantee quick service and a ready smile. In the USA it is different; the bar staff expect to be tipped.

Where to drink

In whatever country one finds oneself it is advisable to be very careful when selecting somewhere to drink. I even found a public house in North London, frequented mainly by Irishmen, where me and my English accent were not exactly greeted with open arms.

In Harare, Zimbabwe, I wandered into the *Masassa* beer hall one hot afternoon for a much needed Lion beer after a long-winded discussion with the First Secretary at the British High Commission. It was not long after Zimbabwe had celebrated its independance so I was not too surprised by the hostile glares I received from the all-black clientel on entering the place. I ordered my beer in a rather pronounced English accent just to inform all and sundry that I was not a Rhodesian. I was advised later that my accent and the fact that I was wearing a suit and tie, and not the mandatory shorts sported by the white locals, had probably saved my skin. It seems I was the only known white man to have used that particular bar since the war in Zimbabwe had ended.

Nigerian beer halls, on the other hand, are friendly but noisy places. The Nigerians' normally exuberant nature is even more noticeable when he has had a drink. There is a tale often told of two Nigerian businessmen who, on meeting unexpectantly in a London street, were arrested for causing an affray. The bobby on the beat could not understand that the violent back-slapping and grappling was a fairly normal Nigerian greeting.

It is not unusual to be asked "Hot or cold?" if one requests a bottle of Guinness in West Africa. A local preference is for a bottle that has stood on the shelf in a temperature around ninety degrees Fahrenheit. It certainly saves on washing-up as the only thing to do on opening the bottle is drink as quickly as possible. The contents erupt with such force that pouring into a glass is impossible.

Expatriates on the other hand go to great lengths to ensure their beer is cold and a common trick is to keep the glasses in the fridge along with the bottles. After a long hot day driving around with the temperature and humidity in the nineties there is no more welcome sight than the condensation forming on a cold glass of Harp lager as one reposes in a comfortable armchair of an air conditioned hotel lounge.

I recall lying back in a chair of a hotel in Ibadon after a particularly frustrating day installing radio equipment at the airport. Mac and I had just poured out the contents of a litre bottle of Harp into two glasses and were teasing our tastebuds as we waited to savour the first sip. Our contemplation was suddenly interrupted by a Nigerian sitting himself down at our table. I noticed Mac frown as the white haired stranger, who was smartly dressed in a grey suit, white shirt, and red tie, opened his attache case.

Mac sat up. "Look man, I don't care what the bloody hell you are selling, we are not interested." It had been one of those days.

The old man stood up and very slowly closed his case, removed his gold rimmed glasses and placed them in his top pocket.

"Sir," he said, with immense dignity, "I am selling nothing. I am the Bishop of Ibadon." And he was!

I saw him later in the evening and explained that Mac was normally a polite and friendly person and that his outburst was the result of a strenuous day when our efforts had accomplished nothing. We were soon forgiven and after treating the Bishop to his favourite tipple of gin and water, we were proudly shown photographs of him at a Buckingham Palace garden party.

At Benin, a large town 120 miles to the east of Lagos, I had the occasional drink with the Oba, or local king. He had been educated at an English university and was always immaculately dressed in a suit and tie whenever I happened to see him. I was, therefore, very much surprised some months after I returned from a trip to Nigeria to see on a David Attenborough TV programme the Oba with a painted face and bedecked with feathers. The programme was supposed to depict a typical day in the life of the local community. To this day I do not know whether the Oba conned Mr Attenborough, or whether Mr Attenborough conned the public. It was certainly nothing like a normal day that I ever experienced in Benin.

In Nigeria there is no need to enter a bar or beerhall if one needs a drink. The locals make a brew from the sap of a species of palm tree which is known as palm wine or "orogoro". The purveyor of this commodity usually transports it in gourds which festoon his bicycle and sells it in measures from an old can. An empty Carnation milk tin is the favoured measure. Non-locals are strongly advised to resist any temptation to sample this very potent drink. Drivers are also warned to give any "orogoro" seller a wide berth when encountering one pedalling his way, and his wares, along the highway. They have the habit of sampling the stock at every potential sale. Whether this is to prove the merchandise is palatable, or is a perk of the job, I am not quite sure. Palm wine trees are jealously guarded and woe betide anyone attempting to help himself to a free drink.

In the USA bars seem always to have the curtains or blinds drawn. I cannot recall ever having been able to look out of the window while in a bar in the States. In fact, it's difficult to see much inside an

American bar as the level of lighting is kept to a minimum. This makes the identifying of dollar bills very difficult as they are all the same size and colour irrespective of value. It is not only in a bar that mistakes can be made with dollars; I once gave a barber a ten dollar tip for a five dollar haircut.

Another thing to beware of in the USA is "happy hour". Whereas in a British pub the beer is at a cheaper rate (£1 a pint for example), in the States it is usually two drinks for the price of one. If you order one drink you will receive two. If you do what I did and ask for the same again, two beers, you will get four. I can recall, vaguely, an evening in Barnaby's Bar at the Holiday Inn, Rochester, when I had a table full of untouched bottles by the time happy hour had ended. And a tidy collection of empty ones.

Some bars in the USA restrict the amount of drinks that they sell to customers, a maximum of only two drinks being sold to each person in some establishments. I am sure the Civil Rights brigade would have something to say if this system was ever tried in the UK. However, it does operate in some places in the States and applies equally to tourists as to the locals. So, if you are thirsty, just find another bar, there are always plenty around.

In "dry" countries such as Saudi Arabia and Kuwait, new arrivals are sometimes surprised at the amount of alcohol available. At one time, when drinking was strictly controlled, the only drink to be had was the home-made *sadiqui,* or *flash* as it was known in Libya. This was pure alcohol made by fermenting a saturated sugar solution with yeast and then distilling the resultant "mash". Unless the distillation process was carefully regulated the final product could contain quite deadly mixtures of ethyl and methyl alcohol, with obvious serious consequences to the consumers. Home brewed beers were also popular in the seventies and eighties but the last time I was in Saudi Arabia there was no shortage of imported beers and spirits to be had on the black market.

In Arab countries that allow drinking one is very likely to come across *arak,* or *arrack.* This is a very potent drink made from coco sap, rice, grapes, or dates. Strangely, the word *arak* means sweat in Arabic. I always found that after a couple of snifters the last thing on my mind was running about working up a sweat!

For some strange reason, probably dehydration, drinking on an aircraft seems to have twice the effect as drinking alcohol in the local back home, so always drink in moderation when flying.

We are all becoming increasingly aware of the number of "air rage" cases now being reported, not to mention other examples of uncharacteristic behaviour occuring a mile high in the air. Although myself a dedicated beer drinker on *terra firma,* I stick to vodka and plenty of tonic when flying. If nothing else, it cuts down on the necessity to visit the WC which is invariably engaged for most of a routine flight

Drinking on board ship can also have a strange affect on the unwary. It is quite easy to sit in the saloon and swig beer from Dover to Calais, or Harwich to the Hook of Holland, but walking out into the fresh air on arrival can have quite a catastrophic affect on one's legs. Sea air and alcohol is a heady combination.

The British pub is of course unique to the UK but replicas can be found wherever tourists are likely to be. Before the troubles in the Lebanon there used to be a very English Rose and Crown in Beirut. Paris, New York, and every Spanish resort now have "British" pubs.

The most peculiar watering holes must be those of Norway. I visited one in Oslo where, after purchasing the beer at the bar, I was obliged to take it and place it on one of a row of chest-high counters that ran along the room. There were stools provided but no tables. Conversing with another customer was like having a chat over the garden wall, if you were lucky enough to find someone willing to talk to you. The Norwegians are definitely serious drinkers.

For any pool players travelling abroad, you will be pleased to find that in most bars the tables are free to play upon, however, be aware that the rules may well be different. In the UK the rules were changed so that the breweries could make a profit from the tables to add to the vast amounts they already make on the drinks.

In Germany, especially in Hamburg, they still have bars that are out of bounds to women. A notice on the door will state *"Frauen Verboten",* but on looking in, one could be forgiven for thinking that the notice had been misread as the bar will usually be crowded with beautiful looking young ladies. The snag is they may look like young ladies but are, in fact, young, and not so young, men!

In Muslim countries, and also Israel, you may find the bars will shut during religious holidays but hotels will usually serve drinks in the lounge or on the patio. In Israel during the Feast of the Passover bread and dairy products are not available even in hotels. It only lasts a couple of days and you should find something on offer in the restaurant to your liking during this time.

The price of drinks can vary enormously depending on where you are. In Nigeria, with the Niara now almost worthless, a litre bottle of Harp lager works out at just pennies a pint. In Djerba, Tunisia, a single Johnnie Walker Black Label in a hotel costs around £10.

It is advisable to drink the local brews whenever available as they are invariably much cheaper than imported brands. Many breweries such as Heineken, Budweiser, Guinness, and Carlsberg have arrangements with local companies to produce in a country under licence. In Europe there is no shortage of local brews, many of which, like Stella Artois, are exported in vast amounts to the UK. There are also North African countries such as Morocco, Tunisia, and Egypt that produce excellent local beers and lagers. And the Gold Star of Israel is definitely worth a mention. In the south of Africa, Lion and Castle beers are excellent and South African cider is well worth a try.

Dining out
Having eaten in restaurants and hotels far more often than at home for the past thirty years I no longer consider eating out a recreation, but I realise others do and so have decided to include a few lines on the subject, although I was tempted to include it in the chapter on health after some of my experiences.

I have already mentioned how I contracted food poisoning after eating scampi in the USA and ended up in hospital for the night, and how I had a similar experience after eating paella in the Bristol Hotel in Beirut but, fortunately, did not get admitted to hospital on this occasion although I was restricted to my hotel room for three days.

The moral of the above misfortunes is to be extremely careful when eating seafood anywhere in the world, but there is no reason why you should not seek out and sample the local cuisine wherever you happen to be. To list all the local dishes I have eaten over the years is impossible but I am willing to list a few of my favourites.

Pea and ham soup	Netherlands, especially in Amsterdam.
Clam chowder	Northern states of the USA.
Seafood gumbo	Mississippi delta, USA.
Stuffed vine leaves	North Africa.
Pepper fish/steak	West Africa.
African stew	South Africa.
Sausage and rösti potatoes	Switzerland.
Kotelet mit brat Kartoffeln	Germany.
Moules marinière	France, Belgium, or Morocco.
Tilapia (fish)	Africa, especially Lake Victoria.

If you do wish to sample the tilapia from Lake Victoria I suggest you do it very soon as this fish is rapidly disappearing from the lake. Some bright spark had the notion to introduce the Nile perch to the lake as a source of food. However, this fish is a ferocious predator and can grow to a length of two metres. Having only the local fishermen to contend with the perch has proliferated and is having a devastating affect on the indigenous fish population of the lake which were predominantly vegetation feeders. The result is the lake is now almost completely overgrown with water hyacinth which makes catching the perch even more difficult, thereby further exacerbating the problem. Ironically, it is firmly believed that the water hyancinth was introduced to the area by a British colonialist attempting to improve his garden.

Fortunately, the tilapia is readily available across most of Africa, where it originated, but is now to be found in the Far East and also in the southern states of the USA. If you do come across it anywhere, it is well worth sampling.

Any of you venturing to the USA will find that restaurant portions are more generous than those usually encountered in the UK. At a bowling alley in Rochester, on requesting a pizza, I was asked how many plates I required. "One" I replied, which seemed to surprise the man. He shrugged his shoulders, walked off, and then returned with a pizza the size of a dustbin lid!

Before I close on the subject of eating out I would like to pass on a bit of advice that was given to me years ago. Never eat in a restaurant that is advertising for staff. It is trouble enough to get served with a full compliment of workers, how much worse will it be if they are understaffed?

One last bit of advice, if expecting to find a good English breakfast abroad, forget it. I am still looking after almost fifty years of travelling. You may find a decent bit of bacon, or a passable sausage, or a nice fresh egg, but the chances of finding all the ingredients of a good breakfast, including a proper slice of toast are minimal. I usually settle for scrambled eggs as it is almost impossible to mess that up.

Other pastimes

Although, as previously stated, my main recreation when working abroad tends to be the local hostelry, I have been known on occasions to enjoy other pastimes. These are normally nothing more adventurous than a casual sail around the bay and a bit of sunbathing.

There should be no need for me to repeat my warning on the danger of exposure to the sun overseas as already expressed in the chapter on health, but I feel I should mention the fact that those idyllic beaches can hold unknown horrors for the unwary tourist.

Before plunging into the sea anywhere be sure it is safe to do so. Even on UK beaches people drown every year because they were not aware of the dangers that can lurk in the most tranquil of seas. If there are flags and lifeguards about be sure to heed them.

West Africa is becoming more popular every year and, although the sea is warm and the beaches beautiful in the Gambia and Sierra Leone, the Atlantic Ocean can get very rough indeed. The wash from some of the huge tankers plying these coasts can be terrifying for small children or inexperienced swimmers, and can arrive completely unannounced.

I will assume that anyone who chooses to go on a climbing holiday knows a lot more about this activity than I do so I will not presume to give advice. However, many people choose to go on walking holidays, the majority of whom are mature enough to know the pitfalls that can await in mountains and forests, but how often do we see on the TV news people having to be rescued after getting into difficulties that for the most part are completely avoidable? Bad weather does not miraculously appear from nowhere; it has generally been forecast at least twenty-four hours ahead.

If you are going off into the woods, mountains, or the desert tell the hotel or guesthouse where you are staying where you intend to go so that in the case of an emergency at least someone will know you are missing and can commence searching for you while there is still a chance of finding you alive. Have a chat with the locals about your intended route and ask their advice. If a certain party of Brits had done that in Oman a few years ago they would not all have perished having a picnic in a wadi which was known to be subject to violent flooding after rain in the hills.

In these days of cellular phones there are now a lot less places where one has no contact with the rest of the world. In many overseas locations, especially the USA, it is possible to hire a GSM telephone for a week just by producing a credit card. This may be safer and cheaper than taking your personal phone with you, plus the fact a hired one is guaranteed to work on local networks.

As someone who has gone to sea professionally as well as an enthusiastic amateur, I am utterly convinced that there should be some form of driving test before people are allowed to take any type of craft on the water. It seems ludicrous that someone who cannot see past the end of the bow, has a history of heart trouble, and drinks to excess, is perfectly entitled to take a motorboat with twin outboards on to a highly congested beach without any form of licence or insurance.

It is equally ridiculous that a respectable South African engineer, who has driven heavy goods vehicles with a clean licence in his own country for twenty-five years, is told his licence is not valid in the UK. The mind boggles!

On the subject of driving licences, do not forget to check with the travel agent that your licence is valid in the country or countries you intend driving in. As previously mentioned, most countries will allow holidaymakers to drive on their national licence but, for extended stays, an international licence, or in the case of Libya, a local licence will be required.

One pastime that was for a long while uniquely British, the game of darts, has become increasingly more popular worldwide over the past ten years. I have played in dart leagues in Saudi Arabia, Egypt, Morocco, Oman, and Zimbabwe so, if you do enjoy a game of "arrows", don't forget to pack your darts. Beware, the rules may be a bit different to the ones you are used to.

For years I thought potholing to be the most inane and boring activity ever to be considered a pastime. What on earth possesses grown men to go ferreting about in the bowels of the earth? Is it some subconscious desire to return to the womb? Even train spotting has more going for it. At least it is carried out in the open air.

However, for pure lunacy, white water rafting has to take the biscuit. How anyone can consider it to be an enjoyable experience roaring down the rapids of the Colorado or Zambezi strapped to nothing more substantial than a glorified air bed, I do not know. And as for bungy jumping — words fail me.

Do note, that if you do intend to get involved in such pastimes as listed above then it is your duty to inform your insurance company back home. Many far less adventurous diversions such as gliding and skiing are not covered by an ordinary accident policy.

For the normal minded would-be sportsman there is nothing better than to be able to spend time overseas in a more temperate climate than that encountered in the British Isles. It is wonderful to wake up day after day knowing that after the work has been done one will be able to take a dinghy out on the bay, play tennis or a round of golf, or dive into clear, warm waters.

Most airlines are quite willing to carry sports equipment such as golf clubs, bicycles, and skis but I do not advise attempting to transport your own kayak. Most large holiday resorts have sports complexes where you will be able to hire the necessary equipment if you have no wish to take your own. Skuba diving is becoming increasingly popular but, whereas you can pack your wet suit I should imagine you will have great difficulty trying to get your air bottles on board an aircraft.

For the less active sportsman, do not be afraid to go and watch one of the local teams in action. In the USA I became quite a fan of the Rochester Redsox baseball team even though, on arrival in the town, I had no idea how the game was played.

Most sports arenas overseas are far more family orientated than those to be found in the UK so you need have no fear of taking children of any age to watch.

In any third world country you will find much more dedication to sport than is now found in the western world. To many a child in the slums of Calcutta and Rio De Janeiro cricket and football respectively are the only hope they have of a decent future. In Bangladesh for eight months of the year most of the country is under water but it does not deter them from playing cricket. One often sees makeshift games where the space between the wickets is the only dry patch. The outfielders are often up to their waists in water in the rice fields. With that kind of dedication it is no wonder that a country as poor as Bandladesh can now compete with the rest of the world.

All over the African continent wherever there is half an acre of flat, uncultivated space you can find goalposts, usually fabricated from branches or bamboo, with a dozen or so barefooted urchins chasing enthusiastically after a half deflated football which has seen better days.

I think it is no coincidence that the standard of British football has steadily declined as schools have been forced to sell their sports grounds in order to subsidise the education of pupils. Until the mad urge in the UK to build on any piece of greenery larger than a snooker table has been curtailed, I fear we will have to depend on foreign players to raise the standard of the national game.

What is ironic is the fact that the youngsters of today in Britain wear tracksuits and trainers, and sport their favourite football teams' latest shirts, all of which cost a fortune, but they rarely own a pair of football boots. As a young lad the first thing I looked for on Christmas Day was a present the size of a shoebox hoping it was my new pair of boots. Maybe now that certain footballers are earning astronomical salaries and living the lives normally attributed to pop stars, we may find more young men kicking a ball and be willing to pick up a cricket bat instead of a base guitar. I sincerely hope so, the future of home-grown sport depends on it.

For those wanting to see something different there is always camel racing in the Middle East, ostrich racing in South Africa, and the sheep Grand National in North Devon! I'm sure the Aussies will get around to kangaroo racing one day, if they have not already.

When the opportunity arose I also did a bit of sightseeing, but I tried to seek out the less visited sites. In Zimbabwe I did visit Victoria Falls on a few occasions but much preferred the Chinoyi Caves. Just descending in pitch darkness into the bowels of the earth was daunting enough, but when a fellow trogalodite struck a match and I found myself on a staircase less than a metre wide, hacked out of the rock with nothing in the way of a handrail, I began to doubt my own sanity. Eventually we found ourselves beside a pool of almost black water looking up at a circle of sky a hundred metres or so above us. Our guide then regaled us with tales of how the local chiefs would throw people down into the depths as a source of amusement.

In Saudi Arabia I also visited caves, one of which the locals claimed was the one that Judas Escariot hanged himself in after he had betrayed Jesus. It seemed to me a heck of a long way to go from the Garden of Gethsamane just to commit suicide.

I have visited Niagara Falls but have also been fortunate enough to see some spectacular falls in the Drackenburg Mountains of Lesotho. In fact, I have rather unpleasant memories of Niagara. The first time I saw them I ended up the same night in an American hospital with food poisoning after eating half cooked scampi, as I mentioned elsewhere in the book.

If you ever go sightseeing in Tokyo or any large Japanese city, be sure to have a good guide. The Japanese name very few of the streets in their towns, and also are inclined to keep them short and not very straight. I was told it was because the old towns grew up outside castle walls and the owners of these buildings objected to any roads leading straight to the gates, as this would be very helpful to any invaders. Some local businessmen even have maps printed on the back of their calling cards to help would-be clients find them.

Airsmiles 6

An aircraft was flying through very turbulent weather conditions and the passengers were being severely buffeted. To calm them down the flight attendants wheeled out the drinks trolley.

"I'd like a brandy" said a nervous passenger in the first row.

Moving on, the stewardess asked the man sitting behind her what he would like. Holding tightly to the arms of his seat he replied "Just give me whatever the pilot's drinking."

CHAPTER SEVEN

Shopping

Bartering

No matter where one travels, and for whatever reason, there will come a time when it is necessary to purchase something. It could be something as insignificant as a bus ticket, or if you are foolhardy enough, something as dramatic as illicit diamonds in Botswana. Wherever, and whatever, it is very helpful to know a little of local protocol where trading is concerned. For example, credit cards are still totally useless in large parts of Africa, as is a Marks and Spencers charge card in Saudi Arabia (having Jewish connections M and S is banned, and also Coca-Cola).

You will not be able to buy wines and spirits in Saudi Arabia, Libya, or Kuwait, or any pork products. As someone who loves a full English breakfast, it has always amazed me that the one single thing the Jews and Arabs can agree on is that all products from a pig are unclean. This from people who eat goats, which must be the animal equivalent of the dustcart. I have seen these creatures devouring everything from empty cement bags to old shoes.

The goat meat that I have seen has a horrible greyish colour to it, and certainly does not smell as appetising as a rasher of bacon or a pork chop when being prepared for the table. I do not know if sheep and goats can cross breed (a *shoat* or a *geep?*), but I know that in the Middle East there are strange varieties of both animals to be found. I was once informed the way to differentiate between the two is by their rear ends. A sheep's tail hangs down, a goat's tail curls up. Unless you know better?

Also, do not bother to go looking for a gold or silver crucifix in the Maldives. Anything appertaining to any religion except Islam is forbidden. In fact, it is an offence to attempt to bring a Bible for your own personal use into the country and you stand the risk of having it confiscated on arrival.

Sadly, the age-old custom of bartering is fast disappearing from the Middle East and large stores in the cities now have notices which state unambiguously "Fixed prices operate in this establishment". Twenty years ago it was great fun to go to the local *souk* (market) in Saudi Arabia, sip mint tea presented by the proprietor, and haggle over an Italian carpet or a Japanese wall clock.

On one occasion in Riyadh, because of my ability to speak a little Arabic, I was called upon to accompany a member of the judo club to the market where he wished to purchase mattresses which he intended sewing together to form a wrestling mat. After spending half an hour negotiating a price for a mattress I informed the judo man of the price agreed.

He nodded his head and said, "Tell him I'll have twenty."

Instead of being overjoyed at the large order the trader leaped in the air beating his chest and all but pulling his hair out. He then informed me he could only afford to sell one mattress at such a ridiculous price. His family would starve if he sold twenty so cheaply! We then proceeded to renegotiate a price for twenty mattresses, a process that took another half an hour. He did, however, supply me with a free rope to lash the final purchases to the roof of my Landrover.

Timing is very important when shopping in Muslim countries. In Saudi Arabia the shops once closed completely during prayer times. I was not the only expat to have found himself thrown out onto the pavement with half a haircut when the *mutawaeen* (religious police) rapped on the barbershop window. The call to prayer comes five times per day in Muslim countries so be sure to keep an eye on the clock when planning a shopping excursion.

In Spain the shops close every day from 1.30 – 4.30 p.m. when the workers go off for a *siesta,* supposedly a sleep in the heat of the day. Most, however, can be found in the nearest *taverna* having a coffee or something stronger.

In France also, most shops close for a two-hour lunch break, and sometimes even longer. The one thing I never quite became used to when working in France was just how much was consumed at lunchtime. I very quickly stopped taking wine with lunch as it made me quite drowsy in the afternoon. At Cazaux, working with the French Air Force, I was amazed to find they had a wine bar in the hangar. My old Chiefy in the RAF would have had forty fits if he had seen it.

In Holland they have *Dutch Auctions.* Where else? Unlike a normal auction where prices start low and work up, in Holland they start high and keep dropping until someone makes an offer. It stops a lot of messing about as the first shout gets whatever is on offer. If you wish to see one of the auctions in action, they happen every morning at the flower markets. Mind you, you will need to be up at the crack of dawn to see them.

While on the subject of Holland, or The Netherlands as the locals prefer it to be called, while there have a look around the antique furniture markets. Some very good bookcases and *bombe* chests can be picked up remarkably cheaply.

After a day's work or sightseeing in Saudi Arabia, Libya, or Kuwait one cannot relax in a bar, or take a trip to the cinema or local dancehall, so a walk around the souk is a recognised form of relaxation. The old souks in Riyadh were exciting places where the smells of camphor, spices, perfume, and local confectionery mingled together in an almost intoxicating aroma. Goods on sale included such diverse items as ancient firearms, Marie Therese Dollars (genuine and fake), ex-army greatcoats, gold jewellery, and musical instruments. It was the latter that took a group of us into the souk in 1969.

Swimming pools were unknown in the Kingdom in those days so we made our own amusement. Many of the lads took the opportunity to learn to play the guitar or something equally musical. On this particular occasion we were mulling over a collection of flute-like instruments. Dave, a gangly young man from Devon, picked up one of the objects on display and attempted to blow it. After two or three attempts and not succeeding in producing a single toot he called to the proprietor. "Here, sadiq, this flute, mush quois, no work".

The gnarled old Arab shuffled over, his bright little eyes peering short-sightedly from either side of his hooked nose. He took the proffered flute and placed deep into his left nostril the end that had just been between Dave's lips. Whatever melodious tone was emitted was completely eclipsed by Dave coughing and spitting for all he was worth.

One thing that I found had not changed on my last visit to Saudi Arabia is the fact that it is appreciated if one makes an effort to learn a little of the language. Years before, when there was nothing much to do after work, I had attended Arabic lessons, and what I learnt has stood me in good stead on many occasions. An effort to learn a few words of the language before visiting any country will not go amiss.

Places to shop
With the proliferation of supermarkets across the globe, once inside one of these establishments it is extremely difficult to tell exactly where one is. A Lidl's store in France or Germany is little different from one in your local High Street. Woolworth, Marks and Spencer, McDonalds, KFC, and a host of other businesses can be found on almost every continent. However, I for one do not see the point of shopping in a British or American store if I am in Africa or Asia. I like to sample the local products.

The funny thing is, what we consider local products such as shirts and underwear purchased in Marks and Spencers are more than likely to have been produced overseas. When I was in Morocco in 1997 I saw two huge M and S lorries loading up every week outside a shirt-manufacturing outfit in Rabat.

In Dhaka, Bangladash in 1999 when my luggage went off to Melbourne without me, the office boy volunteered to go and buy me some essential clothing at the local market. For less than £10 he came back with two pairs of underpants, two vests, two pairs of socks, and two shirts. The following day I purchased two pairs of trousers and had them tailored to fit for only £12. Almost identical clothing can be purchased in M and S or British Home Stores in the UK, but at five times the cost!

I especially like having a haircut abroad. In many Middle East countries I have had my eyebrows and nose hair clipped at no extra cost. I can just imagine the reply I would get from my local barber if

I asked him to attend to my nasal cavities! It is a strange thing about barbershops, no matter where on earth you visit they all look practically the same.

In Nigeria, as in many other countries, it is possible to do a lot of shopping from the relevant comfort of one's car. Even on the North Circular Road in London I have purchased a bunch of roses whilst stopped at the traffic lights. In Africa at traffic lights, and whenever the traffic comes to a stop, which is very often in downtown Lagos, one is persistently accosted by people selling newspapers, magazines, bread, cassettes, video tapes, watches, flashlights, toys, plastic goods of all descriptions, and cooked snacks. In fact, almost anything can be bought along the roadside. It comes as no surprise to me when the Nigerian sprinters do so well in the Commonwealth and Olympic Games. I have seen young lads carrying a mountain of goods keeping pace with sports cars in which they had espied a likely customer.

When driving in the bush in many parts of Africa one can purchase fresh fruit, vegetables, fish, and a variety of game for ridiculously low prices. Bananas have a completely different taste when picked and eaten fresh from the palm, as do mangos and peaches.

Be careful when buying game in the bush in Nigeria. Congo "meat" is actually the giant West African snail, and "rabbit" is a large bush rat, as is "grasscutter". Although it takes a lot of nerve to first try these local delicacies they can be very good. I especially liked the Congo meat and always bought a clutch of live snails whenever the opportunity arose, although the mess they made crawling around the back of the vehicle on the journey back to town was disgusting.

The houseboy, nowadays referred to as the steward, would prepare and cook the snails. I do not know the whole process for preparing them but do know that he smashed the shells and soaked the bodies overnight in a bucket of water to which he added something he called "lime". The following morning the bucket would be covered in a green froth, but by the time I returned from work the snails would have been cooked with herbs and tomatoes and served with pounded yam — delicious. In texture they resemble sheep's hearts but the taste is completely different.

Native art is widespread in Africa, and well worth purchasing. Again, the best bargains are bought out of town, direct from the artisan if possible. In almost every country you will find examples of wood and stone carving, painting, and cloth manufacturing and decorating. In the north of the continent leather goods are an excellent buy, whereas in Zimbabwe and Malawi some beautiful copper items can be found.

While we were in Zimbabwe my wife started a collection of soapstone animals. Soon we had almost every animal that I had seen in the country, plus a lot I had not. The animals were all of a very high standard. Unfortunately, my wife could not find a hippopotamus to her liking. For some strange reason the carvers never seemed to get their legs in proportion, probably because, very sensibly, they only went near the animals when they were in the water.

My wife's quest for the perfect hippo became well known around town in Harare. So well known in fact, that I was once arrested and charged with "malicious damage to a hippopotamus" after accidentally breaking a leg off a rather pathetic looking carving which had been thrust into my hands by an over-zealous street trader. When he refused to take it back I placed it on the ground at his feet, at which point the leg fell off.

I retired immediately to the bar of the Monomotapa Hotel and ordered a Castle beer. Shortly after I was approached by a member of the local CID to whom I had been reported. Given that I was working for the government (and to avoid any hassle) I offered to pay for the carving, only to find that the price had gone up by ten zim dollars.

"If the price is going to go up with every missing leg, you might as well break them all off and make forty dollars" I expostulated. But, refusing to pay the extra, I was promptly arrested and taken to the police station.

At the copshop, all hell was breaking loose. As Robert Mugabe was chairing some international meeting over the weekend, he had ordered a clean-up of the streets. Not with a dustcart but a Black Maria dashing about rounding up prostitutes. There were dozens of women at the station all protesting their innocence. Some claiming they were in town looking for work, some trying to return home from work, others on shopping trips, and such like. (It later transpired that one of the women arrested was the wife of an American diplomat!)

My arrival, carrying a briefcase and wearing a suit and tie, caused instant pandemonium. Some thought I was a lawyer who might be able to help. Most decided that I was a potential client and I was propositioned a dozen times on my way to the charge sergeant.

Explaining to him that I had been wrongly arrested, I took the three-legged hippo from the aggrieved carver and waved it in front of the sergeant's face.

"Would you seriously be pleased if I took such a decrepit piece of Zimbabwean art back to Britain?"

He appeared to be close to agreeing with me as I placed the animal on the counter. At which point, another leg fell off. I collapsed laughing, as did a dozen ladies of the night. The carver howled in anguish, and the sergeant threw me in the cells.

At the High Commission in Stanley Avenue the following morning, the powers-that-be failed to see the funny side. I was "advised" to pay the carver for the hippo and I complied. I kept one of the legs as a souvenir and gave the rest of the animal a decent burial in the garden. I still have the leg over twenty years later.

My wife did eventually find a hippo to her liking.

That episode was bad enough, but the most embarrassing purchase I ever made was in, of all places, the UK.

I was home in Devon, on leave from Libya, when I received a telephone call asking me to go to London because a piece of test equipment was urgently required by the air conditioning department. As "an extra two days leave" was mentioned in the conversation, I agreed and went up to London to purchase an Annimeter from a company recommended by the engineers. The suppliers explained it was sensitive equipment and better hand-carried than shoved in the hold as baggage. As it was only a small package, about a foot square, I thought nothing of it.

All went well until I came to security before boarding the aircraft.

Hand luggage was searched, with the usual fuss about my tool kit, and this was twenty years before the infamous *9/11* incident.

"What's in the box?" enquired a female security guard who could have stepped straight out of Prisoner of Cell Block H.

"A meter" I replied.

"Well, I'd like to meet her" came the strange request.

"Meet who?" I asked, completely at a loss, and now conscious of a long queue forming behind me.

"Annie" was the reply.

I looked at the box I was clutching to my chest. Only one word was printed on all four sides – Anni. The awful truth dawned on me. She thought I was carrying some kind of sex aid. And judging by the sniggering going on behind me so did a lot of other people.

I hastily placed the box on the counter in front of her. "Go ahead" I said, conscious now that I was blushing furiously, "It's only a measuring instrument."

As she withdrew a penknife from her pocket and commenced to slowly cut the masking tape, a horrible thought struck me. I had never actually seen the meter, it had been presented to me already wrapped. What if it was a set-up? I had never had anything to do with the suppliers before. Did they provide sex aids? Had that lousy shower back in Tripoli pulled a fast one?

The following ten seconds were the longest of my life. I dare not look into the box. I watched the security guard's face. When I saw the look of disappointment wash over her countenance I breathed again. She closed the lid and pushed the box towards me. "Okay, you and your friend Annie are free to board."

I know to this day there are a dozen passengers who were convinced I carried a blow-up doll to Libya.

It was not surprising that I was suspicious of the package, as I had been the victim of my colleagues' wicked sense of humour in the past. On a shopping trip in town one of the lads had bought his wife a kaftan but was not sure it would fit her or not.

"Here Bill," he said to me over a beer one night, "you're about the same height as my wife." (I am closer to five feet than six feet.) "Do you mind putting this thing on so I can get an idea of the size?"

Do not ask me why, but I eventually agreed in the privacy of his room to don this dress. You can guess the rest. As soon as I had it on, the door burst open and half a dozen of the swine were snapping away with polaroid cameras! I was buying beer for a week before I retrieved all the evidence of my foolishness.

Mind you, my embarrassment was nothing compared to a case I

read about recently. A British woman tourist set off the security alarm at Athens Airport. On investigation it turned out that her husband had insisted on her wearing a metal chastity belt! I must have led a sheltered life; I did not know such things still existed.

Shopping in the USA
Shopping in the USA for the first time can be very surprising as no one wants cash. The credit card rules supreme. I once attempted to pay for a burger and coke with a hundred dollar note in a McDonalds — the manager was called. I felt like a criminal as the note was held up to the light and scrutinised. He asked me half a dozen times if I had anything smaller. When I pulled out my wallet and revealed dinars from Libya, riyals from Saudi Arabia, niara from Nigeria, and malote from Lesotho, he must have decided I was a harmless nut and not a felon and I was finally allowed to pay in cash.

Beware that in the USA the price marked on an article is not necessarily the price you will be asked to pay at the cash desk. A tie marked $5.50 in a J. C. Penney store eventually cost me over six dollars by the time Federal Tax, State Tax, and God alone knows what other tax was added.

I can never take American dollars seriously being that they are all the same size, irrespective of value, and I find myself using it like Monopoly money. As has previously been mentioned, I once gave a barber a $10 tip for a $5 haircut. I had intended to give him $1 but having made the mistake did not have the nerve to ask for the $10 back.

Much as it behoves me to praise the Americans for anything after the way they have mangled our beautiful language and forced all the worst aspects of their way of life upon us (I refuse to use the word culture), I have to admit our supermarkets could learn a lot about customer relations from the US model. At the checkout counter in the States a cheerful individual packs your carrier bags, which are, incidentally, always free, and after loading them into a trolley willingly pushes it to your car in a huge car park which always has available spaces. He will refuse a tip saying he is paid to do what he does, but will accept if you offer twice. He then wheels away the empty cart bidding you "have a nice day".

Compare that to a typical UK supermarket where a surly, gum chewing individual flashes your items past the bar code detector at the speed of light. Your shopping is then hurled towards where you stand wrestling with the carrier bag dispenser. Eventually you manage to free a bunch of a dozen or more that some fiendish swine has glued together in the factory that manufactured them. By the time you have retrieved one and succeeded in finding the opening your goods are in a heap in front of you. The checkout person is now sat staring at the ceiling drumming his/her fingers on the till while a queue of shoppers wait impatiently to be subjected to the same torture.

You now have to crane your neck to see the total that has been rung up as the display is always mounted for her benefit not yours, and unless you ask she is not going to tell you. Having paid and received your change screwed up in the till receipt, you are now in mortal danger of losing a few fingers as the next client's beer and dog food are despatched frantically in your direction.

Having eventually packed the trolley you find that whereas, five minutes ago, it went quietly to wherever you pushed it, it has now developed an aversion to the car park. It will go in any direction but the one you want. You give up pushing and decide to drag it behind you, thereby leaving yourself open to attack from all its metal mates being shoved at you by late shoppers envious that you have completed the horrors that still await them.

If buying electrical goods in the USA for use in the UK or Europe, make sure that they are dual voltage, 120/240 volts, and 50/60 cycles, otherwise you will have the additional expense of buying a transformer in order to operate the goods when you return home. Also beware, items designed to run at 60 cycles will not operate properly on UK supplies.

Another problem could be with the warranty. Goods purchased in the USA, or other countries, may not be covered by the guarantee when imported into the UK.

Everyone is aware of the power of advertising. We are accosted almost everywhere we go by the huge multinationals such as Coca-Cola, Pepsi, Marlboro, Carlsberg, and Budweiser. There is relief from the constant barrage in some Middle East countries for religious reasons, and other countries on health grounds. However, on my considerable travels around the globe, the three items that can be found anywhere in Africa or Asia, and other continents as well are Carnation Milk, Lipton Tea, and Nivea Cream. Carnation Milk is so well established in African countries that an empty tin is a recognised measure of some commodities such as peanuts.

I have seen the familiar yellow sachets of Lipton Tea in tiny shops in the Keys of Belize, in the villages of Bangladash, and in Sabha, a town on the rim of the Sahara Desert. In Saudi Arabia, after writing paper, Nivea Cream was the best selling item in the camp shop. The dark blue tin, which was available in many different sizes, could be found in almost every bedroom. It was the only defence for exposed flesh from the hot winds, liberally sprinkled with sand, which never ceased to blow at Riyadh. Everyone reeked of the stuff, whether he was a rough handed rigger or a shiny suited secretary.

These items have worldwide popularity but can never be considered as the most widely advertised.

In the USA you can shop for anything twenty-four hours a day. I have had a wonderful breakfast just outside the airport in San Francisco at five o'clock in the morning. I have bought perfume in New York at two o'clock in the morning. There are dry cleaners open at midnight that will clean your suit while you wait. There are even pawnbrokers open at this time in case you have to hock your watch to get a taxi home. If you are too drunk to go home there are cinemas where you can hide in the darkness until you sober up again. You can even find a prayer meeting going on, where you can ask forgiveness for your sins and get a bowl of soup for your trouble. America has a lot going for it, it's just a pity there are so many Yanks there!

It is not only in the USA that credit cards are becoming more and more popular with holidaymakers as a way to obtain cash and goods abroad. Here are some words of advice on the use of cards.

Make sure you know your PIN number and the emergency number should your card be stolen or lost. You will need your PIN number to make purchases in some overseas countries.

Check that your card is acceptable at your intended destination before travelling. Your issuer will be able to supply this information.

Check the expiry date – it is easily overlooked, as I know from personal experience.

Check the total after every transaction and beware that commas are often used where we use decimal points.

Keep a record of all transactions to compare with your bank statement on your return home.

Finally, normally you will be charged commission on all money obtained from overseas cash machines.

Money changing
Although shops in the USA may seem to have no interest in paper dollars, everywhere else in the world they are readily accepted. Taxi drivers in almost every capital city will know immediately the cost of the fare in dollars if asked, and are usually quite honest with the exchange rate. In Cairo, if wanting to see the sights including the pyramids at Giza, ask a taxi driver for a quote to hire by the day in dollars. I had an air conditioned Mercedes which took me to the national

museum, the Pharonic village, the City of the Dead, waited while I had lunch at Cairo's MacDonalds, then drove me to the pyramids in the relative cool of late afternoon, and all for less than the price of a coach trip to Giza quoted at the hotel.

Although the American dollar is readily acceptable in most parts of the world be very careful when obtaining them. They are amongst the simplest of currencies to forge and it is estimated that around the world £7 billion worth of counterfeit dollars are circulating. When the Iraqis invaded Kuwait they looted the banks only to find that hundreds of millions in US currency was counterfeit. Many foreign countries refuse to accept American notes of $100 and above, so to be on the safe side use only low denomination notes.

All over Africa, with so many countries having financial difficulties, there is a ready black market for dollars and sterling. In Libya in 1998 the official exchange rate was $3 to the Libyan dinar, but on the black market one could sell a dollar for three dinars. In Nigeria and Zimbabwe there are even more favourable rates to be had, but I advise extreme caution if tempted to make a few pounds this way. It is illegal and local authorities come down very hard on people caught carrying out such activities.

A recent proclamation from the Nuremburg Institute for Biomedical and Pharmaceutical Research (only the Germans could dream up a title like that) stated that 90% of the euro banknotes in circulation show signs of having been in contact with cocaine. They further state that this is because they have either been used to sniff the drug or handled by cocaine dealers. However, some cynics claim the notes were deliberately contaminated so that people would lose their inhibitions when spending them. I believe the beer-sodden notes in my local have been having the same affect on me for years!

There was a time when shops overseas were very different to British shops but with the power of multinational marketing and the growth of supermarkets, it is now possible to feel equally at home shopping on any continent. By the very nature of their produce, greengrocer shops abroad still have to differ from those at home. Butchers and bakers also differ as there is not much call for a pork chop in Tel Aviv or pumpernickle in Telford. There is, as I have mentioned earlier, one establishment that hardly differs whether one is in Peterborough, Panama, Paris, or Pretoria and that is the hairdressers. The only difference between them is the colour of the hair on the floor and the language in the tattered periodicals.

Most travellers probably know that there is a branch of Marks and Spencers in Paris but how many are aware that one can shop in Harrods in Beunos Aires, at Tesco's in Prague, at Sainsbury's just a hop and a skip away from the Pyramids in Cairo, and at Boots in Bangkok? It seems the High Street is never far away no matter where you are in the world.

Saving on shopping
As is equally true in the UK, it pays to shop around before buying and there are places to avoid like the plague unless money is no object. Such a place is the hotel shop. Whatever is on display in the hotel can always be purchased far cheaper if you are prepared to go and look for it. This especially applies to the dreaded mini bar now omnipresent in the rooms of larger hotels. The prices of the contents, nuts and chocolates as well as various drinks, are many times the cost encountered in a normal shop or market.

If you have a predetermined idea of what you wish to take back with you, such as a wooden shark from Belize, a soapstone carving from Zimbabwe, or a silver replica of a bicycle taxi in Bangladesh, then start negotiating with a local trader from the first day of your trip. By visiting for a couple of minutes every other day and doing a bit of haggling it is amazing how much will have been knocked off the asking price by the end of your stay. If you can get two or more suppliers to compete for your custom, then so much the better.

The souks and bazaars of North Africa and the Middle East are relatively honest places, but, as everywhere else, there are disreputable traders willing to take advantage of the unwary. Just take a walk down Oxford Street a week before Christmas!

Make sure that what is wrapped up so securely for you is the actual article you have paid for. Be especially careful if you are just passing through on a coach trip or as a passenger on a pleasure cruise. The traders know you are not going to be able to come back the next day and complain, when, on unwrapping your purchase back at the hotel or on board, you discover that instead of a silk scarf for mother-in-law you have a cotton tea towel.

Not long ago I visited a street market in Amsterdam and saw a very nice jacket at a reasonable price. Having tried it on and received my wife's assurance that it fitted perfectly I purchased it. The trader then proceeded to wrap it for me. On returning to the hotel I hung it in the wardrobe. The following morning when I put it on I had the shock of my life. I had shrunk five sizes overnight! My wife collapsed in a heap laughing while I stood there wearing this jacket that reached to my knees. It was so big I was never able to find anyone large enough to give it to. It went to a charity shop eventually. I expect some

Japanese sumo wrestler is the proud owner of it now. Needless to say, when we returned to the market the following day the trader who had sold it to me was nowhere to be seen.

Never buy videotapes or CDs from market traders abroad. It's a 99% certainty they will have been copied from an original or recorded from a satellite receiver and will be completely unusable. Be careful of brand name material if the prices are too good to be true. Chances are they are fakes. Chinese made "Omegas" and "Seikos" are now to be found everywhere.

There is also a huge market in counterfeit perfumes and designer clothing to be found all over the globe at the present time. I was surprised to see so many refugees in the Balkans wearing the latest in Hilfiger, Calvin Klein, Benetton, and other fashionable clothing until it was pointed out to me that it was all counterfeit material that had been seized by British Customs and later donated to various charities. It is comforting to know that it is not just the insurance companies who are benefiting from the ever-increasing rise in crime.

What, and what not, to buy
I think most people are now aware that there is a ban on ivory trading so would not attempt to import a pair of tusks, and I am relieved to no longer see elephant feet sold as wastepaper baskets. However, small items of ivory such as bracelets are still available, and legal, so I will leave it as a matter between you and your own conscience as to whether or not you wish to spend money on such articles.

Tortoiseshell, hard and black corals, rare woods, and some sea shells are also banned from international trade but are still readily available in countries such as Greece, Turkey, the Caribbean, and parts of Africa.

It would take another publication for me to list what is legal to import and export from each individual country, but I will give just this one piece of advice; if it's living, leave it, and that applies to plants as well as creatures.

There are, in fact, 25,000 banned species in the Convention on International Trade in Endangered Species.

Many items of food are restricted, and not only pork products to the Middle East. The import of fruit, vegetables, and meat products is stringently controlled in the USA. To prevent any hassle do not attempt to carry any food into the country. If you do have an apple or two left at the end of your flight I would leave it on the aircraft.

Imports of meat and some other food products are also banned by the British Government. Signs at my local airport, Exeter, warn of dire consequences awaiting anyone foolish enough to be caught carrying a black pudding into the country. Replica guns and knives are OK in the cargo hold but not black puddings!

Very attractive china and earthenware goods can be obtained almost everywhere overseas and usually for a reasonable price. If you wish to use them as ornaments then go ahead and buy them. If, however, you are thinking of serving food on them, think again; the paint could very well be unsafe. A lot of heavy metals such as manganese and chromium are used in the glazing process in many Asian and South American countries. What these would do to your microwave oven I can only imagine.

Gold is well worth buying in Middle Eastern countries as it is usually sold by weight at the market price for the day. No extra, or very little is added for the workmanship involved in the object. I have had jewellery valued in the UK at more than double the price paid in Libya and Saudi Arabia.

Gold coins can also be a good purchase. Amongst the most popular for investors are the Kruggerand of South Africa and the US American Eagle. These coins are both 91.67% pure gold. They are, however, eclipsed by the Canadian Maple Leaf that weighs in at an impressive 99.99% pure gold. It is believed to be the most popular of contemporary bullion coins.

Before flying off on holiday acquaint yourself with the prices of goods in your local supermarket, you may find it is not worth burdening yourself with duty free purchases on the way home for what money, if any, you will save.

The following list may help you decide what to take home from your holiday:–

Arab countries – Gold, jewellery, leatherwork, brass.
African countries – Indigenous art, precious stones.
Europe – Clocks, watches, clothes, wine, perfume.
South and Central America – Indigenous art, silverware.
USA – With the present exchange rate of the dollar, just about everything is cheaper than in the UK, especially clothing and electronic goods.

Well, that's about it as far as advice goes, you are now on your own. It is impossible to prepare for all emergencies but, hopefully, what you have gleaned from this publication will help you deal with most of the problems you are likely to encounter. All that remains now is for me to wish you *bon voyage*. Happy landings.

Airsmiles 7

A young male passenger was pleasantly surprised to find the check-in desk adorned with Christmas decorations during the holiday rush.

"Why is there mistletoe hanging above the desk?" he asked expectantly.

The beautiful attendant smiled sweetly. "So that you can kiss your luggage goodbye" she replied.

APPENDIX

Useful telephone numbers
Major airports:

Aberdeen:	01224 722331
Alderney:	01481 822624
Belfast City:	028 9093 9093
Belfast International:	028 9448 4848
Birmingham:	0121 767 5511
Blackpool:	01253 343434
Bournemouth:	01202 364235
Bristol:	0870 1212747
Cambridge:	01223 373737
Cardiff:	01446 711111
Coventry:	024 76762220
Dublin:	(00 353 1) 8141111
Dundee:	01 382 643242
East Midlands:	01332 852852
Edinburgh:	0131 333 1000
Exeter:	01392 367433
Glasgow:	0141 887 1111
Guernsey:	01481 237766
Humberside:	01652 688456
Inverness:	01667 464000
Isle Of Man:	01624 821601
Jersey:	01534 492000
Leeds/Bradford:	0113 250 9696
Liverpool:	0151 288 4000
London-City:	020 7646 0000
London-Gatwick:	0870 0002468
London-Heathrow:	0870 0000123
London Heliport:	020 7228 0181
London Luton:	01582 405100
London Manston:	01843 825063
London Southend:	01702 608100
London-Stansted:	0870 0000303
Lydd:	01797 320000
Manchester:	0161 489 3000
Newcastle:	0191 286 0966
Newquay:	01637 860551
Norwich:	01603 420653

Plymouth:	01752 204090
Prestwick:	01292 511000
Sheffield:	0114 2011998
Shoreham:	01273 296900
Southampton:	02380 620021
Stornoway:	01851 702256
Sumburgh:	01950 461000
Teeside:	01325 332811

Car ferry services:
Brittany Ferries:	0870 536 0360
Condor Ferries:	0845 345 2000
DFDS Seaways:	0870 533 3222
Eurotunnel:	0870 535 3535
Hoverspeed Ltd:	0870 524 0241
Norfolkline:	0870 870 1020
P & O Irish Sea:	0870 242 4666
P & O North Sea:	0870 129 6002
P & O Portsmouth:	0870 242 4999
P & O Stena Line:	0870 600 0600
Red Funnel Ferries:	0870 444 8889
Sea France:	0870 571 1711
Stena Sealink:	0870 570 7070

Major airlines:
Aeroflot:	020 7355 2233
Air Lingus:	0845 084 4444
Air Canada:	0870 524 7226
Air China:	020 7630 0919
Air France:	0845 0845 111
Air India:	020 8560 9996
Air New Zealand:	020 8741 2299
Alitalia:	0870 544 8259
Austrian Airlines:	0845 601 0948
British Airways:	0845 779 9977
British Midland:	0870 607 0555
Cathay Pacific:	020 8834 8888
Easyjet:	0870 600 0000
Finnair:	0870 241 4411
Gulf Air:	0870 777 1717
Iberia:	0845 601 2854
Japan Airlines:	0845 774 7700

KLM:	08705 074 074
LOT:	0845 601 0949
Lufthansa:	0845 7737 747
Luxair:	01293 596633
Malaysia Airlines:	0870 607 9090
Malev (Hungarian):	020 7439 0577
Nigeria Airways:	020 7629 3717
Olympic Airways:	0870 60 60 460
Qantas:	0845 774 7767
Ryanair:	0871 246 0000
SAS:	0845 607 2772
Swissair:	0845 601 0956
TAP:	0845 601 0932
United Airlines:	0845 844 4777
Virgin Atlantic:	01293 747 747

Useful Websites

www.airflights.co.uk
www.airlinenetwork.co.uk
www.airlinewarehouse.com
www.airmiles.co.uk
www.aito.co.uk
www.allezfrance.com
www.americadirect.co.uk
www.annualpolicy.com
www.anztravel.co.uk
www.archersdirect.co.uk
www.asia-direct.co.uk
www.astburytravel.co.uk
www.asthma.org
www.austravel.com
www.autoroutes.fr
www.aviatours.co.uk
www.avionholidays.co.uk
www.avro.co.uk
www.ba.com
www.baa.co.uk
www.balkanholidays.co.uk
www.bargainholidays.com
www.bcponline.co.uk
www.bedbreak.com
www.blueskyholidays.com
www.bon-voyage.co.uk
www.bridgetheworld.com
www.bridge-travel
www.britanniaairways.com
www.brittanyferries.com
www.bruneiair.com
www.budget.co.uk
www.businesstraveller.com
www.camp4less.co.uk
www.canadatravelcentre.co.uk
www.canadianaffairs.com
www.cantabrica.co.uk
www.cathaypacific.com
www.cheapflights.co.uk
www.cheznous.com

www.cityvacations.net
www.comebackalive.com
www.condorferries.com
www.consorttravel.com
www.cruisecontrolcruises.com
www.crystalski.co.uk
www.cunard.co.uk
www.dh.gov.uk
www.dialaflight.com
www.direct-holidays.co.uk
www.directline.com
www.directski.com
www.discovercruises.co.uk
www.discoveregypt.co.uk
www.discovering-europe.co.uk
www.doh.gov.uk/traveladvice/emerg
www.easyjet.com
www.ebookers.com
www.evanstravel.com
www.excelairways.com
www.expedia.com
www.fco.gov.uk
www.ferriscoachholidays.co.uk
www.ferrysavers.com
www.firstchoice.co.uk
www.flexicover.com
www.flightcentre.co.uk
www.flightsearchers.co.uk
www.floridabyphone.co.uk
www.flybmi.com
www.flyingfear.co.uk
www.flyingwithoutfear.info
www.franceguide.com
www.freedomaustralia.co.uk
www.gatewayholidays.co.uk
www.goinglobal.com
www.gulfairco.com
www.holiday.co.uk
www.holidayautos.co.uk
www.holidayoptions.co.uk
www.hoteldirect.co.uk
www.hotelsabroad.com

www.hotfootholidays.com
www.iberiaairlines.co.ukh
www.indigoholidays.com
www.insureandgo.com
www.intrepidtravel.com
www.islandcruises.com
www.jetsave.co.uk
www.journeylatinamerica.co.uk
www.journeywise.co.uk
www.klm.com
www.kuoni.co.uk
www.lastminute.com
www.latedeals.com
www.leadingcruiseagents.co.uk
www.lonelyplanet.com
www.lunnpoly.com
www.maltabargains.com
www.manos.co.uk
www.mercurydirect.com
www.netflight.com
www.nudirect.co.uk
www.oceanvillageholidays.co.uk
www.odesseyholidays.com
www.olympicholidays.com
www.onestepholidays.co.uk
www.placestostay.com
www.pocruises.co.uk
www.portland-direct.co.uk
www.preferredhotels.com
www.premiercover.com
www.questtravel.com
www.rail-breaks.co.uk
www.ramblersholidays.co.uk
www.readersdigest.co.uk
www.regaldive.co.uk
www.roughguides.com
www.russiantravel.co.uk
www.ryanair.com
www.skyscanner.com
www.solosholidays.co.uk
www.spanish-harbour.co.uk
www.specialvillas.co.uk

www.sratravel.co.uk
www.sunstarleisure.com
www.sunways-direct.com
www.teletextholidays.co.uk
www.thisistravel.co.uk
www.thomascook.com
www.thomson.co.uk
www.thomsonflights.com
www.thriftwaytravel.co.uk
www.tourist-offices.org.uk
www.tourspain.es
www.trailfinders.com
www.travel.com
www.travelbag.co.uk
www.travelcare.co.uk
www.travelcitydirect.com
www.travelhealth.com
www.travelmag.co.uk
www.travelmood.com
www.travelocity.co.uk
www.travelpack.co.uk
www.travelplanners.co.uk
www.travelsphere.co.uk
www.travelsupermarket.com
www.tropicbreeze.co.uk
www.virginholidays.com
www.vjv.com
www.wallacearnold.com
www.westernair.co.uk
www.whitehall-leisure.co.uk
www.wild-dog.com
www.windstarcruises.com
www.yahoo.co.uk